FLAMING ARROWS

Allen,
Thanks for
your heart!

Rul

Flaming Arrows: Collected Writings of Animal Liberation Front Warrior Rod Coronado

First published in the United States in 2007 by IEF Press

ISBN 978-0-9842844-5-0

Warcry Communications was formed in 2009 to arm those fighting in defense of all life.

For information, submission guidelines, bulk requests, or general inquiries, please contact:

www.VoiceOf TheVoiceless.org

info@voiceofthevoiceless.org

INTRODUCTION

By the time I first heard of Rod Coronado, he was already in prison. Rod had been sentenced to 57 months for an accomplice role in an A.L.F. arson at the Michigan State University fur bearer research facility. The arson was part of a multi-state arson campaign to destroy the fur industry dubbed Operation Bite Back. Although Rod was sentenced only for being a conduit for materials taken from the lab, the FBI (and activists who could read between the lines) believed that Coronado orchestrated the entire campaign: seven arsons and lab break-ins in five states.

Before long I would find myself a fugitive wanted for A.L.F. actions, just as Rod had been years before. He had already been released from prison, and in one of my infrequent meetings with above-ground contacts, someone passed me a tape of Rod Coronado's speech at the 2000 Environmental Law Conference. His words of continuing the fight no matter the sacrifice brought me a small amount of peace in a difficult time. I listened to the tape often.

Several years later and still a fugitive, I slipped into the back row at one of Coronado's talks given at a conference surely attended by undercover FBI agents. (I would eventually learn from my own talks that the back row is where the FBI usually sits.) As I faced a potential life sentence for mink releases, one of his lines from the podium that day brought solace:

"Going to prison is like going to the DMV: it's just something you have to do."

Rod would go to prison three more times (as of this writing), as the FBI targeted him ruthlessly for speaking in support of the A.L.F. To prevent future prosecutions when it appeared the feds were not going to rest, Rod eventually accepted a global plea agreement which made it impossible for the government to prosecute him for past crimes. For the first time, he was able to speak freely about his role in past A.L.F. actions, including every Operation Bite Back raid. The product of his subsequent confessionals would become Coronado's biography: *Operation Bite Back*, published in 2009. The story provides the most detailed account to date of Rod Coronado's extensive history in the A.L.F.

Operation Bite Back, at Coronado's direction, introduced a new level of strategy to the Animal Liberation Front. For the first time, the typical A.L.F. hit-and-run single-target raid was forgone for a multi-target campaign to destroy linchpins in a weak industry. Going after feed suppliers and research centers, Operation Bite Back went for the fur industry's Achilles heel, and aimed for structural collapse.

As an A.L.F. model, Operation Bite Back will never die. While the fur industry still remains, the next generation of earth warriors will take inspiration from Operation Bite Back's blueprint: trusted friends, a car, minimal equipment, and a plan to deal death blows to an industry through arson at a few well-chosen targets. The model works to cripple an industry by striking at components of its support structure, operations often more vulnerable and easily erradicated than the businesses they underpin.

To offer a brief editorial, I struggled with including the essay "When The Weak Link Breaks", a column about my co-defendant Justin Samuel. When I first read it in 2001, I interpreted it as promoting a "bear no malice" attitude towards informants. Yet despite a degree of ambiguity to the essay, I trust Rod's message was not one of forgiveness for those who have worked to imprison animal liberators.

For this re-release, chapters from *Memories of Freedom* edited out of the first edition have been restored. And a 1996 prison letter has been repositioned beside a 2006 prison letter from a later sentence, juxtaposing Coronado's earlier politics with his more recent revisions.

These writings have brought inspiration and instruction to a generation of daytime activists and nighttime saboteurs. The burden falls on us now to raise the words of *Flaming Arrows* from mere subcultural relic, to battle cry before the next advance.

"Now you must take the risks rather than cheer on those who have walked before you."

For Liberation,
Peter Young

BI on to fax man in ALF raid

BY KEN OLSEN

right 1992, Moscow-Pullman Daily News

Oregon animal rights activist
be distributed the Animal Liber-
Front press release after the
p's August raid at Washington
University.

at the FBI is wrong in blaming him
the raid, especially since no law en-
cement agencies have questioned
i, says Rodney A. Coronado, of the
dition Against Fur Farms. The raid
volved the release of mink, coyotes
l mice and resulted in $50,000 to
00,000 worth of damage to U.S. De-
rtment of Agriculture offices located
WSU.

"The press release just showed up on
my doorstep," Coronado says. "I had no
previous knowledge of it."

Coronado said in a interview this
week he was in Pullman visiting
friends in August when the release appeared. He admits he went to Kinko's
in Moscow the morning after the raid
and faxed the release to the Associated
Press office in Spokane. That's at least
one of the things law enforcement may
be using to tie him to the raid.

Police and FBI agents compiled
sketches of the man and woman who
paid for the fax, based on interviews
with Kinko's employees, and distributed the sketches nationwide. The
sketch of the man looks somewhat like
him, Coronado says.

But he was alone and reports that he

was accompanied by a woman are
false, he says. Reports that he and two
women composed the press release on
computers at the Moscow Kinko's are
untrue, too.

If distributing the press release was
against the law, Coronado says he'll
take the rap. But he doesn't think he's
getting a fair break from the FBI,
which is telling people he was in on the
WSU raid, though it has never interviewed him, he says.

An FBI search warrant affidavit says
Coronado "was responsible for the destruction of animal research facilities at
WSU on Aug. 12-13, 1991," he says. Coronado was mentioned briefly in the affidavit, which was filed by the FBI in

connection with its investigation of a
Maryland woman who is believed in-
volved with an ALF raid at Michigan
State University in February, he says.

That declaration of his guilt, without
due process, violates his Constitutional
rights, Coronado says. "It doesn't seem
to be in the spirit of freedom that this
country was founded on to judge some-
body without a trial."

There is no warrant out for Coronado's arrest and he has not been indicted for the WSU raid, or raids at
Oregon State University and an Edmonds, Wash., mink feed manufacturer, an FBI spokesman says.

Coronado isn't exactly a suspect, he's
a "person of interest," the spokesman

See Raid page 3A

The "Case" Against Rod Coronado:

A Legal Memo on the Green Scare by Ben Rosenfeld

This article was originally posted on a number of independent media websites and was then reprinted in the April/May 2006 issue of the Earth First Journal. It was written prior to Rod's August sentencing.

*T*he federal government has been salivating to put Rod Coronado back in prison since he got out in 1999 and later refused to repent for his role in a 1992 arson at a Michigan State University animal research lab. Federal officials have publicly branded Coronado as a leader of the Animal Liberation Front (ALF), even though the ALF is apparently non-hierarchical. However, he has been an unabashed advocate of property destruction in defense of animals, and the new charge against him—for delivering a speech three years ago in which he explained how the incendiary devices used in the Michigan arson were made—is a flimsy pretext to punish him for his radical views.

The government's targeting of Coronado is part of a broader witch hunt against radical environmentalists and self-identified "green anarchists"—those who merge ecology, animal rights and anarchism into a vision of freedom and sustainability for all living beings. After Coronado's arrest, US Attorney Carol Lam stated in an official press release, prejudging the case for the public: "Teaching people how to build explosives in order to commit violent crimes is unacceptable in civilized society. There is no excuse for it." And so, through sophistry and syllogism, the government has transformed speech into violence.

On December 13, Coronado was convicted in Arizona for peacefully attempting to disrupt a US Forest Service mountain lion hunt (see EF!J March-April 2006). After Coronado's conviction, Assistant US Attorney Wallace Kleindienst told reporters that Coronado is "a danger to the community. ... I know he wasn't tried here for being a violent anarchist. This trial wasn't about Rod Coronado being a terrorist, but he is one." Kleindienst thus revealed the government's two ulterior motives for going after Coronado: One, it has a vendetta against him personally, and two, it has quietly embarked on yet another war against an abstract concept—anarchism.

The new case against Coronado is as stark an attack on free speech as this country has ever seen. Measured against any historic test of free expression, Coronado's behavior—that is, his speech—was alarmingly protected and uncriminal.

On July 30, 2003, persons unknown torched an apartment complex under construction in San Diego, California, causing millions of dollars in damage. The day afterward, Coronado flew to San Diego to lecture at a previously scheduled event. In response to a question from an audience member, Coronado—who has been a public figure on the environmental lecture circuit since his release from prison— demonstrated how someone had constructed a non-explosive, incendiary device out of a plastic jug filled with gasoline to commit the Michigan arson for which he did his time. The government does not suspect, and has not accused, Coronado of any involvement in the fire set the day before his speech.

The Supreme Court has carved out three famous exceptions to free speech: the "fighting words" exception (Chap-Hnsky vs. New Hampshire), the obscenity exception (Miller vs. California), and the "clear and present danger" exception (Brandenburg vs. Ohio). However, each exception is extremely limited. As Justice William Brandeis eloquently wrote in 1927: "Fear of serious injury cannot alone justify suppression of free speech.... It is the function of speech to free men from the bondage of irrational fears.... No danger flowing from speech can be deemed clear and present, unless the incidence of the evil apprehended is so imminent that it may befall before there is opportunity for full discussion.... The remedy to be applied is more speech, not enforced silence."

But playing "gotcha," the government has charged Coronado under an obscure, anti-First Amendment law that makes it "unlawful for any person to teach or demonstrate the making or use of an explosive, a destructive device or a weapon of mass destruction... with the intent that it be used for, or in furtherance of, an activity that constitutes a federal crime of violence." This law has yet to be challenged on constitutional grounds.

The Department of Justice (DOJ) reportedly has used this law only four times—twice now against dissidents. In 2003, Sherman Austin, the then-20-year-old founder of the anarchist website www.raisethefist.com, pleaded guilty to it in order to avoid a possible 20-year sentence just for hosting and linking to another website on his server, which provided crude, Anarchist Cookbook-style information on bomb-making (see EF!J November-December 2005). The same information is widely available elsewhere. Austin otherwise had nothing to do with the site he linked to. But according to the government's theory of the case, Austin's anarchist beliefs and the political content of his website furnished the requisite intent. Thus, the government substituted other speech for intent, thereby nullifying the only part of the statute that required something more than mere speech. Austin served one year in prison. So much for the First Amendment.

The arrest of Coronado occurs in the midst of a new Green Scare, in which the FBI would have us believe that eco-saboteurs—who engage in property crimes such as arson and vandalism, and studiously avoid causing injury to people—constitute "the number one domestic terrorism threat," as FBI Deputy Assistant Director for Counterterrorism John Lewis told a Senate panel on May 18, 2005. Apparently, according to the FBI, the threat is greater than that posed by neo-Nazis, systemically brutal and racist police forces or Al-Qaeda.

Since then, the FBI's Joint Terrorism Task Forces—multi-agency units operating out of every FBI field office— have mercilessly harassed numerous environmental and animal rights activists by conducting paramilitary-style raids on their homes; seizing computers, papers, photos and other personal belongings; subpoenaing scores of people to grand jury inquisitions; engaging in electronic surveillance; dispatching informants to demonstrations; and even planting informants in people's homes.

In January, the DOJ unsealed a 65-count indictment against 11 alleged eco-saboteurs (the number has since grown to 15) accused in a series of arsons committed under the banner of the Earth Liberation Front (ELF). Even though the ELF disavows violence and no one was hurt, the government has branded them terrorists, thereby cheapening a term that, by its very mention, affects policies and budgets. In some cases, the DOJ is seeking life terms for the young activists, while the same crimes, if committed to defraud insurance, would land them a few years in prison.

The Green Scare picks up where the Red Scare left off—with the FBI bruised and reprimanded by Congress for engaging in illegal break-ins, wiretaps, frame-ups and even assassinations of members of targeted political continued from previous page groups. Now, Congress is the enabler of such FBI dirty tricks, not so much legalizing them as laundering them through the passage of flagrantly unconstitutional laws like the USA PATRIOT Act—reauthorized by Democrats and Republicans alike—and the looming, retroactive legalization of the National Security Agency's illegal domestic spying program.

Both the Red Scare and the Green Scare fuel and are fueled by a hysterical hatred for a broad political philosophy—communism, and now anarchism—caricatured as a tangible threat casting its shadow over the land. Thus, anarchists—a diverse group of people from all walks of life, who generally agree that most government structures are repressive, that people shouldn't be greedy and that we should support one another—are reductively drawn as bomb-throwing lunatics. Massachusetts Institute of Technology Professor Noam Chomsky, who has lobbed many books at the public, is an anarchist. George Orwell was one too.

Also in January, with the arrest of three suspected eco-saboteurs in Auburn,

California, the FBI revealed that it is investigating the "anarchist movement," writ large. Special Agent Nasson Walker disclosed in an affidavit that the FBI had embedded a paid informant with the suspects, recruited when she was only 18 or 19. The FBI had dressed her up as a medic and dispatched her to participate in numerous peaceful, large-scale protests. Needless to say, most if not all of the people she interacted with (politically organized with, treated medically and lived with) were not plotting crimes of violence or sabotage. Yet the FBI can claim—with a whiff of legitimacy, even—that it has the right to engage in such intimate espionage and dragnet-style policing because ex-General John Ashcroft relaxed the Attorney General Guidelines to permit widespread snooping. Originally created to protect the public from repressive tactics after the exposure in 1971 of its COINTELPRO operations, the guidelines now permit the FBI "to go anywhere the public can go" in Ashcroft's words, without any foundation of suspicion that a crime is afoot. Undoubtedly, the FBI did not blow "Anna" the informant's cover without leaving other agents in the field... and in political meetings, in decision-making positions in groups and in people's homes.

Agent Walker's affidavit is further revealing of the FBI's backslide into politically motivated investigations. It references "anarchist" or "anarchism" 26 times in its mere 14 pages. In it, Standing up for people's rights of free expression, whether one agrees or disagrees with the message, is fundamental to a free society. the FBI seems obsessed with the anarchist "lifestyle," anarchist literature and anarchist gatherings. These invocations of dread anarchism add nothing to the scales of probable cause. It is elemental that a person is not guilty by association to an unpopular (or popular) cause. But as a public relations move—in seeking more constitutionally suspect laws, higher bails, more warrants, longer sentences and a bigger chilling effect on progressive activists—the government's projection of a giant anarchist menace is highly effective.

On January 13, the FBI's David Picard plainly admitted on network television that the FBI is again investigating an entire ideology as if it constitutes, a domestic security threat. "One of our major domestic terrorism programs is the ALF, ELF and anarchist movement," he said. "And it's a national program for the FBI." Then, on March 9, FBI Agent G. Charles Rasner revealed at a speech in Texas that Food Not Bombs, Indymedia and "anarchists" are on an FBI "terrorist watch list."

Against this backdrop, it is clear that Arizona Assistant US Attorney Kleindienst, who labeled Rod Coronado a "violent anarchist," was not just spouting personal invective. He was reading from the official program.

Standing up for people's rights of free expression, whether one agrees or disagrees with the message, is fundamental to a free society. As Chomsky put it in Manufacturing Consent, "If you believe in free speech, then you defend speech that offends you, because to only defend speech that you agree with is a function of the commissars of Soviet Russia and Nazi Germany."

To convict Rod Coronado, prosecutors will have to prove that his demonstration created a "clear and present danger" that it would be used toward violent ends, and that he intended as much. In a rational setting, this should not be easy. Coronado's audience probably was not comprised of glazed-over Manchurian candidates, determined to and capable of going out and making violent revolution—if ever such a group existed. Moreover, the construction of an incendiary device from readily available materials, such as a plastic jug and gasoline, hardly constitutes an arcane science. If the term "destructive device" includes items so simple to construct, it might turn out to be too vague to satisfy constitutional due-process standards.

What we know for sure is what the government has already told us: This trial isn't about Rod Coronado being a terrorist. The other thing we know for sure is that while real environmental terrorism goes unabated, forests recede, species go extinct, ice caps melt, and the sea levels continue to rise.

Ben Rosenfeld is a civil rights lawyer in San Francisco, California, and a board member of the Civil Liberties Defense Center in Eugene, Oregon. He was one of the members of Judi Bari and Darryl Cherney's legal team.

DZIL NCHAA SI AN

A WARRIOR'S STORY
OF UNDERGROUND RESISTANCE

*I*n this sacred place that we fight to protect, long before Earth First! warriors occupied the frontlines here, we came to pray. Here where the Earth spirits are strong, warriors of the Apache and Yaqui Nations came. This is where I choose to tell a story of underground resistance to defend the Earth, not the whole story, only what I remember and can now safely tell. It is one small part, maybe only a chapter in what must be a continuing resistance.

It is a long road that brought us to where we are today, like the sun that rises, our resistance follows darkness. We have been here before, and we will be here again. I remember standing on the Dakota prairie, where the blood and bones of many Earth warriors lay, when She first spoke to me. The Awakening. My first realization that this struggle was much bigger than any of us. When I became painfully aware of what it meant to put the Earth first. To not only eschew the anti-nature laws of the Invader, but to aggressively break them in defense of all that we love. The Earth Mother cared not who we were, only that we were willing to defend her.

Monkeywrenching is more than a tactic or strategy, it's the way of warriors. A way of life. The way of the wild and the free. A refusal to allow our spirits to be broken. It is our spiritual duty for that most ancient power in our world, the life giver, our one Mother Earth.

In the Autumn of 1986, after fighting Nordic whalers in the fjords of Iceland and the Faeroe Islands, I came home not to something new, but something very old: human children putting their lives on the line for Earth once more. We were no longer asleep.

Awakened in the night, we attacked the machines destroying Earth. As we liberated ourselves from societal control, we began to become more than a movement. With strong hearts tempered in the dark, with sweat and oil, we became a tribe again. Across North America, monkeywrenching became the answer for those frustrated with the ineffectiveness of working within the system.

Fences were cut, survey stakes pulled, orange flagging removed and sabotage of heavy machinery became the natural reaction when discovered in the wild forests, deserts and prairies we loved. Fanning the flames were allies in the Animal Liberation Front (ALF) who paralleled Earth First!'s guerrilla resistance with arson attacks and animal rescues on the torture chambers holding hostage our animal relations.

The Earth First! Rendezvous became our time to share skills, stories and music.

Like any tribe, our songs told the story of warrior deeds. Darryl Cherney, Dana Lyons, Joanne Rand and others sang of the love and humor our actions reflected. Together we laughed, loved and strengthened our bond to each other and the Earth.

At the 1988 Rendezvous, Dave Foreman hoisted Icelandic saboteur David Howitt and myself up on stage to salute our raid on pirate whalers, welcoming the new generation of eco-warrior, the young anarchistic animal liberationists who also embraced Deep Ecology. Earth First! was changing. It wasn't just beer-swilling red necks for wilderness anymore. The call for Earth defenders made by Abbey, Watson and Foreman was heard by many primed and ready for action outside the traditional ranks.

Like all struggles for freedom, our resistance to evil forces also awakened the attention of the Spirit Hunters. In the Arizona night of May 1989, flares lit the desert sky as federal agents with automatic weapons and infrared goggles surrounded four saboteurs cutting a transmission tower. Although all four were arrested, the main target of this FBI counter-intelligence campaign was Earth First! co-founder Dave Foreman, who was indicted as a co-conspirator.

It wasn't long after this government attack on the radical environmental movement that warriors renewed their raids. In April 1989, inspired by a call for a direct action response to the corporate buyout of Earth Day, Earth Night Action Group downed power lines from a coal-fired generation station in California.

An FBI memo circulated during the investigation revealed the government's fear. "...various activists groups... ALF, Earth First!, Lockheed Coalition, Hunt Saboteurs and the Anti-Nuclear Alliance are no longer fighting amongst themselves because of single issue orientation but have instead banded together, thereby providing a larger number of extremists to draw from in order to commit crimes..." My elder warrior-friend Paul Watson warned that when our struggle began targeting institutions within the United States, we would bring down upon us the total weight of the FBI and other federal law enforcement agencies fighting terrorism. Our struggle was awakening a giant.

The repression of 1989 and 1990 was a historic response to legitimate resistance. The feds began to harass family and friends of suspected eco-warriors, driving a wedge between the underground and above-ground support. Violent attacks against folks like Judi Bari and Darryl Cherney were ignored while the feds concentrated on the enemies of profit and some activists began to cower as grand juries subpoenaed many to testify against colleagues in the movement.

We began as a small group engaging in property destruction, but evolved to a larger network, carrying out large scale raids on universities and corporate targets, costing them millions. Rather than rushing to the newsstands to read of our exploits, we began to cover our tracks. The FBI was constantly on the hunt, waiting for us to make that one fatal mistake that would lead to capture.

I moved to the Siskiyou Mountains and organized attacks, believing one should only be amongst the enemy to raid. Living with the source of my power, the animal people and the wild Earth, I began to renew a vital connection. Alongside the survivors and refugees of humans' war on nature, I saw that all living beings in Creation were nations unto themselves, struggling to raise their families and stay alive in a relentless war that wiped out entire races.

By 1992, the feds were hot on the trail of eco-warrior cells across the West. In April federal agents kicked in the door of my Siskiyou stronghold just days after I had fled. It was time to go underground. I took refuge in the prairies that hid Lakota warriors after their victory over General Custer. It was there that I realized what this struggle was all about. Sleeping with a loaded handgun under my pillow, waiting for the agents of repression to take me away, I gave them power in my fear. I still recognized the US government's ability to control my destiny.

I reached the breaking point. On a long walk on the prairie I prayed and told Creator that even if death lay ahead, I stood with all Creation. On the side of the bobcat and the lynx, the coyote and the mink. It was them I fought for, and I wasn't ready to turn my back now. A gentle wind brought a hawk gliding over, and with his glance I knew I was not alone.

That's when She spoke. I cannot describe it as anything more than love. A flow of energy that reduced me to tears as I awakened to the Spirit around me. "We are here. We have always been here. We will always be here, but there is nothing we can do for you, until you believe in us more than you believe in them. "Suddenly the whole world was alive, and every being in it consciously aware of it's connection to all others. A coyote stared. In its gaze I heard, "Now you are a hunted one. Now you are one of us." At that moment I became aware that all the legends, myths and stories about the Earth and her animal children were true.

A task force of federal, state, county and university police were after us. Grand juries in Oregon, Washington, Montana, Louisiana and Idaho were trying to intimidate us. It was time to show our power. I headed for the Rendezvous. Hiking in 13 miles, I arrived at night to the sounds of the campfire. Standing outside of its glow I waited until I could identify trusted warriors. Within days we were on another reconnaissance mission.

When the government's Animal Damage Control Predator Research Facility went up in flames, stories were told of how the coyotes who could not be rescued helped those who could. A chorus of howls covered the sounds of warriors entering the labs. When cages were being cut, coyotes dug frantically alongside warriors and ran toward the calls of their free cousins. Three warriors went to jail for six months instead of cooperating with the Spirit Hunters. At the height of repression meant to crush us, we demonstrated what it meant to be free.

Two years later I was tackled by federal agents, and in fall 1995, I stood here on *Dzil Nchaa Ziann* praying. That day I would surrender at federal prison to a four-year sentence. The resistance continued. The same month of my imprisonment, warriors struck a fur farm releasing thousands of mink. In September of this year, 14,000 more went free in the sixty-eighth raid on a fur farm since 1995. There have been nearly that many raids on genetically engineered crops. All the federal agents in the United States will not stop more actions of this sort.

The Earth Liberation Front (ELF) burst onto the scene in 1996, demonstrating an ability to raid corporate targets before drifting away as silently as it came. In December 1998, when all legal channels had failed, the ELF carried out a spectacular multi-pronged attack on a ski resort responsible for destroying habitat for the endangered Canada lynx in Colorado. The $12-million act of sabotage harmed no one, and over 80 federal agents have been unable to capture a single warrior.

Daily I pray for our warriors. May they move as swift as the mountain lion in the night and strike as rapidly as the owl. May their footsteps be silent like the lynx, their strikes like lightning. May the enemies of the Earth sleep uneasily, never knowing when or where we raid next.

As Earth warriors, we choose to be participants in the ancient battle between good and evil. On our side stand the waters and wind, and all things wild and of the Earth. On the other side, consumed with greed and in pursuit of power, control and money, stand all the dark forces that lay waste to Her.

One day our animal relations will no longer run from us as if we were enemies. They will know us as friends. Until then, we must continue to demonstrate to them, ourselves and the whole world that we are willing to risk our freedom for them and their wilderness homes.

Some say it's a wild and impossible dream, but I don't want to live in a world without dreams. Dreams are what kept our warrior ancestors alive in their darkest hours, and they will keep us alive in ours. Warriors have to live and love life today if we want to be free tomorrow. The gift we are given is not just for us, it must be shared, as a key to free others. This is where our dreams begin and where generations of warrior dreams continue.

Spread Your Love Through Action

Prison Letter From Rod Coronado

On March 3, 1995, I pled guilty to aiding and abetting a fire at Michigan State University that destroyed 32 years of research intended to benefit the fur farm industry. The Animal Liberation Front (ALF) claimed responsibility for the raid, the seventh in a series of actions dubbed "Operation Bite Back" which targeted fur farms and universities engaged in taxpayer supported research jointly funded by the fur trade. I also pled guilty to one count of theft of U.S. Government property, in particular, a journal belonging to a 7th Cavalry Officer killed at the Little Bighorn near Crow Agency, Montana in 1876. This negotiated plea agreement is the result of a seven year investigation by the FBI into my activities and the Federal Government's continued targeting of indigenous activists who assert their sovereignty and continue their fight for cultural survival. It also is the culmination of nine federal grand juries that have lasted over three years, subpoenaed over sixty political activists, jailed four for six months each, and harassed and intimidated countless others in the hunt for members of the Animal Liberation Front. In return for the guilty pleas, the U.S. Government promises not to seek further prosecution of me in the remaining districts investigating the ALF, nor subpoena me to testify against others suspected of ALF activity. The price I pay for not testifying against my compatriots is a three to four year prison sentence. Prior to the plea agreement, I was the sole defendant in a seven count indictment alleging that I was responsible for a nation-wide coordinated effort to cripple fur farm research and development. With a life-time commitment to protect the earth behind me and in front of me, I must choose carefully the battles in which I fight, and the arenas in which I fight them. Like most indigenous people I am unable to match the limitless resources of the U.S. government in their efforts to incarcerate me, nor am I able to adequately defend myself amidst laws that criminalize the preservation of our sacred mother earth. This is only the latest attempt by the U.S. Government to make an example of those who break free from the confines of legitimate protest. At a time when ecological and cultural destruction is commonplace and within the perimeter of the law, it sometimes becomes necessary to adhere to the higher laws of nature and morality rather than stand mute witness to the destruction of our land and people. I believe it to be the obligation of the earth warrior to never be ashamed of ones own actions, to honor the sacred tradition of indigenous resistance. Therefore, I accept full responsibility for my actions and remain grateful to have had the honor of serving as a number of the ALF as their spokesperson and supporter. With a record of over 300 animal liberation actions and rescues in the U.S. without injury or loss of life, yet thousands of lives spared from the horrors of vivisection and fur farming, the women and men of the ALF remain to me some of the most respected of non-violent warriors in the struggle to save our planet. My role in the raid at MSU was as a non-participant, acting as a conduit for the truth hidden behind the locked laboratory door. While in Ann Arbor, Michigan awaiting instructions I received a phone call from an anonymous ALF member detailing the raid for inclusion into a press release. Later, I received research materials and evidence seized during the raid. These documents would have exposed taxpayer sponsored research benefiting the fur farm industry, and experiments where mink and otters are force-fed toxins and other contaminates until they convulse and bleed to death.

Accompanying these documents was a videotape of the cramped and unsanitary conditions mink and otters endure at MSU's research laboratories. My desire to release this information to the public was much greater than my desire to protect myself from the rabid investigations by the FBI and ATF. Seventeen months later, I was indicted by the Michigan grand jury based on this evidence.

Earlier in the month of February, 1992, I was at the Little Bighorn River in Montana. I went to the sight of the infamous battle and was shocked at this, the only monument I know of that glorifies the loser. In further disgrace to the warriors who lost their lives defending their families and homelands, the monument paints a one-sided story of the conquest of indigenous peoples of the Great Plains by the U.S. military. The truth remains that George Armstrong Custer and his 7th Cavalry were an illegal occupational force trespassing in clear violation of the Fort Laramie Treaty of 1868 to attack peaceful encampments of noncombatants in the heart of the Lakota Nation. The theft of the Cavalryman's journal is a reminder of indigenous discontentment with the treatment of our heritage and culture by the U.S. Government.

Over the last ten years I have placed myself between the hunter and the hunted, the vivisector and the victim, the furrier and the fur bearer, and the whaler and the whale. These are my people, my constituency. It is to them that I owe my life. I have chosen to continue the time honored tradition of resistance to the invading forces that are ravaging our homes and people. Many people have been tortured, murdered and imprisoned on this warriors path, yet we must continue to stand tall against the tyranny that has befallen this continent in the last 503 years. As warriors we must accept that prison awaits those who are unwilling to compromise the earth and her people when we choose to remain allegiant to fellow warriors whose identity remains unknown. We are all Subcommandante Marcos, Crazy Horse and the ALF. Never, ever should we forget that in order to achieve the peace and liberation we strive for, some sacrifice must occur. Unfortunately, history tells us it is almost always us who must sacrifice. This will not be the first time an indigenous person has gone to prison while upholding our obligation to protect our culture, homelands and people, and it most definitely will not be the last. It is with total love that I say good-bye to my earth mother for a little while to enter the concrete and steel prisons the U.S. Government reserves for its discontent citizens. Such rewards await those who must give their lives and freedom to prevent the destruction of the most beautiful planet in the universe, our life-support system, our beloved mother earth. To those who have fought beside me, you will always be my friends and my families, and for you I will give up that which I love the most, my freedom. I will face prison rather than speak one word against those on the front lines of the battle to protect earth. Our relationship is a sacred one, and in your own freedom I pray that you spread your love through action that continues to rescue all that remains wild. Never Surrender!

Though we may never see each other again in the trenches of the struggle for animal and earth liberation through illegal direct action, in my heart I will always hold you closest. Be patient my friends. I have not forgotten those already behind bars, those in traps and in the rifle sights of man's ignorance and greed. It is time for me to hand over my role as a "hero" to the animal and environmental movements to others whose faces are not yet known. To you I give the responsibility to preserve and protect what is left of the splintered nations of others we call animals. In your hands lies the future of this centuries old struggle, in yourselves you must find heroes. Now you must take the risks rather than cheer on those who have walked before you. With a strong heart, the spirit of the earth which is our greatest strength, will never leave you. Carry her spirit well, and shower yourselves in her beauty when in need of true power. I have been brought back home by my people, the Yaqui Nation and it is to them that I now return to satisfy the restless spirits of my grandmothers whose cries I must answer.

Sometimes we are forced to do things we do not like when we are warriors. On this land that I now live where my ancestors are buried, the Great warrior Geronimo sometimes found it necessary to surrender to the Enemy in order to recruit young warriors for future battles. We are a patient people. Never forget the beauty, magic, love and life we all fight so hard to protect and that others have given so much to defend. Our pain and sadness is very real but so is our happiness and joy as we witness the coming Spring. I will always be beside you, and you may always find shelter in my home. I love you all, and in you place the hopes for the rebirth and rekindling of our sacred relations to all animal, people, and creation.

Forever in Your Honor
and in Her Service
Rod Coronado

STATEMENT FROM
PRISON
AUGUST 2006

*D*ear Friends and Supporters,

Some of you know me only by my lectures, writings, actions and statements, some as a father or personal friend. To say the least, these last couple of years have been truly life-changing. I've been arrested twice by the FBI, chased by a helicopter, indicted for serious charges, charged with less serious crimes and, it seems, almost constantly accused of being a terrorist though my actions my entire life have never caused a single physical injury let alone death. That's not to say I haven't done things I regret. I have. But this open letter is meant instead to be a statement of facts in regard to what I now believe. It is partly response to questions raised by past supporters who have always heard me unequivocally support illegal direction actions taken on behalf of the Earth and animals.

I believe there comes a time in everyone's life when we have to honestly ask ourselves why we are here, doing whatever it is we do on this beautiful planet. These last two plus years have surely been such a time for me. All my life I have endeavored to protect the earth and her non-human children we call animals. I still do and always will believe in respecting life be it human or non-human and this planet we all call home. A large part of my personal and spiritual evolution has been in the last nearly five years since I became a parent of a beautiful human child. As a warrior I used to think that having children was an impediment to any struggle for peace and justice. Never could I have been more wrong. I believe our creator chose me to be a

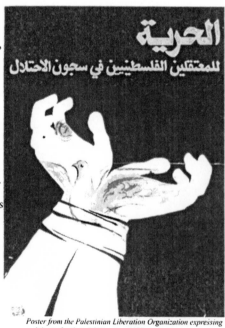

Poster from the Palestinian Liberation Organization expressing solidarity for their POWs, circa 1970

parent of my son because I was a warrior. A man who believed that peace for the Earth and animals could only come through aggressive and sometimes destructive actions.

Raising a child requires a parent to practice the very principles you seek to teach your children. Indeed such is the case with all living beings. I always believed I was fighting to create a better world for all future generations, yet to preserve what I wanted to protect, I chose to engage sometimes in the destruction of property used to destroy life. I still see the rationale for what I've done, only no longer do I personally choose to represent the cause of peace and compassion in that way.

As a parent, I have been forced to realize that violence is everywhere in our society and as a parent I believe in not raising children to accept violence as a necessary evil. I believe in teaching and living peace with the hope that only through example do our children have a chance of escaping a violent future. In my years past I have argued that economic sabotage was an appropriate tactic for our time. Like all strategists I have also been forced to recognize that times have changed and it is now my belief that the movements to protect earth and animals have achieved enough with this strategy to now consider an approach that does not compromise objectives, but increases the likelihood of real social change. Let our opposition who believe in violence carry the burden for its justification, but let those who believe in peace and love practice a way of life that our society sorely needs now more than ever.

A society built around violence cannot stand the test of time. But a life built around the tenets of mutual respect, compassion, peace and harmony can be our only way out of this nightmare. What is won through violence must be protected with violence and I don't want to teach my children that. As long as governments and corporations sanction physical violence any who attempt to stop them with violence will be labeled terrorists.

There is little we can do to change that in light of the media's role and influence over the public's perception. That is only I believe in their ability to label the cause of peace and justice as such. Many people have bravely given their lives and freedom to forward the cause of animals and nature, now let us continue that march in ways that do not allow the opposition to excuse us as terrorists. I believe in promoting the rights of animals and a safe environment through the demonstration of a way of life based on creating sustainability rather than fighting within a system that respects only force and violence. We are fortunate to live in a society that allows nonviolent options. Systems of war and violence shall crumble and we should free ourselves from the rubble while there's still time.

There is no shortage of good works in order to build the society I believe in, only a shortage of those willing to make a life-ling commitment towards creating peace. We know where the dominant society has left us. With less rights and privilege than corporate charters and profit margins. It is now time, I believe, to fend for ourselves and create the democracy denied to us. Time for us to become active in educating our children, in growing and providing healthy food to all, medicine and care giving to those who need it, not just those who can afford it. This is how I believe we create a better world, not through any acts of violence but with great demonstrations of love for each other and all life around us.

I condemn no one forced into a life of self defense through violence, I only pray for another way forward to a lasting peace. There is still time. Time for a government by the people for the people... and earth. But not without the patience and perseverance to build peaceful alternatives rather than short-term strategies that offer too little in the way of long-term change. My position is just the voice of one man on a journey solely his own. I speak for no greater movement though I hope the desires of many. Struggle for me has become a very personal battle. Not only against a legal system intent on imprisoning me but equally important is my personal struggle to be a better human being. To my children, my partner, my community and myself. Because if I can't accomplish peace in my own life, how is it that I can hope to accomplish it on any larger standard?

What our world needs now is a whole lot more love and a lot less violence. Nothing in this world will change overnight. But if we live peace and teach our children well, they might still inherit a world better than ours. Maybe I'm just getting old, or finally thinking about the legacy I will leave behind, but I still have much to live and give and I want to find the commonality between people who want only a safe and happy life for their children. Don't ask me how to burn down a building. As me how to grow watermelons or how to explain nature to a child. that is what I want to grow old doing. Please afford me this. I have fought my battles and continue to fight for mine and my family's freedom. I only want to not be remembered as a man of destruction but a human believer in peace and love for all. May the creator bless and protect us all with the sacred gift of life that is ours to do with as we shall.

For more information about Rod and updates about his court case please visit his official support site:
www.supportrod.org

THE HIGH PRICE

OF PACIFISM

I don't know how it happened, but this past Spring at the Environmental Law Conference in Eugene, Oregon I found myself on a workshop panel on police brutality. I have been on the receiving end of police brutality before, but in general, I avoid direct confrontations with law enforcement authorities and do not believe in confronting a militarily stronger opponent face to face. That is why I personally engaged in ALF activity, because when it comes to fighting an enemy much larger than yourself, the hit and run tactics of guerrilla warfare can create an advantage impossible in conventional warfare.

Too often I hear of nonviolent protesters becoming the victims of violence when they place themselves in the path of opponents who demonstrate a total disregard for their adherence to Gandhian principles of nonviolence. So as I listened to each panel member recounting the instances when police terrorized them and the subsequent legal battles they became encumbered with as a result, I couldn't help but feel that it was sometimes strategically unwise to pursue this avenue of action.

I am not a pacifist. Yet at the E-Law Conference I got the feeling that the majority of attendees believed more in passive nonviolence than aggressive self-defense. So I knew it wouldn't be with wide support for me to say what I believed about my misgiving towards nonviolence in the political climate we find ourselves in today. I told the folks in Eugene that I came from a long line of cop killers. I told them that had it not been for my ancestors' willingness to kill their oppressors I might not be alive today.

In the 1800s and early 1900s to not take up arms against the Spanish, and then Mexican, military often meant the loss of your land, liberty, cultural identity, and even your life. A Yaqui seen was a Yaqui killed, imprisoned, raped or deported and without a willingness to defend yourself, you surrendered control over your own life and that of your family to your oppressor. In a similar fashion, albeit a lot less extreme, I see activists doing the same thing when we religiously adhere to nonviolence and the tactics of civil disobedience in the face of increasingly violent attacks by police.

Don't get me wrong, I prefer the path of nonviolence and it saddens me to see societal attention and change primarily in response only to aggression, but unfortunately, we don't make the rules, we just play the game. Governments rarely respond to whispers, but almost always hear a scream. In such times it becomes necessary for political struggles to reevaluate their tactics and strategies and choose those that result in the least amount of physical violence, not only against our opposition, but equally against ourselves.

To not adapt strategy to changing times becomes counterproductive and when we fail to do so we become partially responsible for the violence that occurs when our nonviolent protesters are encouraged to place themselves in the path of violence prone police. No matter how many nonviolence training sessions you go to or how many books on Gandhi you read, nothing is going to change this police state's policy of using violence against peaceful protesters when they know they have the law on their side and will always get away with it. Which leads to my next point. If we do continue to use nonviolent civil disobedience as a tactic, then we should react appropriately when that tactic is responded to violently. What I mean is self-defense. There is nothing immoral, unethical or wrong with defending oneself. It is the most instinctual response in the natural world. It's genetically built into most every animal and plant and the only thing that prevents us from using it is an institutionalized belief that all physical violence is bad.

Each time we allow violent attacks on us to happen without defensive action we give strength to a dangerous precedent that tells the police that they can get away with literal murder. You need only see what happened to Earth First!er David Chain to believe that. The Pacific Lumber employee who felled a redwood tree on David was never even arrested for the death of this nonviolent forest defender, let alone spent one night in jail like so many nonviolent protesters.

In the 1980s while sabotaging fox hunts in Britain our group was attacked by hunt supporters. I thought I was a pacifist, but when I saw hunt saboteurs defending themselves and the effect it had in showing our attackers that we would not passively take a beating, I abandoned that philosophy for a more pragmatic belief that allowed self defense. When the hunt supporters realized that we'd fight fire with fire they retreated. Their power over us was dependent on our refusal to defend ourselves.

Likewise, whether it during a protest against the World Trade Organization, International Monetary Fund or any other target within the evil empire, when police take advantage of our commitment to nonviolence and victimize innocent young activists exercising their supposed constitutional right to protest, we must retaliate. Maybe not when such a response would further endanger activists, but whenever peaceful protesters are beaten, pepper sprayed, and their civil and human rights violated, we have every right to demonstrate our right of self defense and target the property of our attackers.

Every time a protester is beaten cop cars should burn. Every time an activist is pepper sprayed tires should be slashed and windows of the offending agencies should be broken. These agencies obviously have a total disregard for life, but they sure as hell care about their property. In such a way we are able to preserve our belief in the sacredness of all life while still retaining the ability to defend ourselves.

We must demonstrate our own power instead of always witnessing theirs being used against us and all of natural creation. Even Gandhi said that nonviolence was only appropriate when used against an opponent who respects it. In Northern Ireland it was state violence against nonviolent protesters that forced the resurgence in the Irish Republican Army. In South Africa it was state violence that forced the African National Congress to form the guerrilla army, Spear of the Nation, and in the United States it was state violence that encouraged the growth of the Black Panthers. As Malcolm X said, nonviolence is appropriate with nonviolent people, but if someone attacks you, self-defense is justifiable.

The struggle for animal liberation and environmental defense is about preserving the lives and rights of others, it's not about our own morality, it's about ending a war. To apply tactics that result in long and costly court battles that serve only to divert attention away from animals in labs, fur farms, circuses and the wild and instead see us defending our own rights are strategically a failure. We must only engage in tactics and strategies that focus attention on the truly oppressed, the animal people and their natural homelands.

It's not about feeling good while preserving our privileged philosophies that further separate us from other humans resisting oppression by all means necessary, this fight is about stopping the wholesale slaughter of billions of innocent beings who depend on us for their survival. Let's get over our moral hang-ups and recognize that the fate of the earth and all life upon it calls on a continued escalation in direct action.

WHEN THE WEAK LINK BREAKS:
ON SNITCHES AND SOLIDARITY

A couple of weeks ago I had a conversation with Marlene Samuel, Justin's mother. It was a difficult phone call, and it reminded me of the pain and worry my own mother suffered when I was captured and sent to prison.

Despite my disagreement with Justin's decision to testify against Peter Young, I found it hard to feel anything but sympathy for him and his family. The animal liberation movement should use Justin's case as an example of what not to do when captured for ALF actions.

That Justin could be found, arrested and extradited from another country for opening cages of doomed wildlife speaks volumes about the U.S. Government's resolve to capture and imprison ALF warriors.

In Justin's case, there was once again the spread of misinformation, some from our own movement, that Justin and Peter faced over 60 years in prison (based on the maximum sentence allowable for each indicted offense and not on an actual sentence computation). Justin also suffered the trauma of nearly a year of pre-trial imprisonment and the denial of a vegan diet.

These factors led Justin to agree to testify, hoping cooperation would win him an instant release. A review of court transcripts reveals no such promise. Instead, what is said is that the prosecution and defense attorneys recognized that despite the plea agreement, the sentencing judge would retain the legal right to punish Justin to the full extent of the law. That happened on November 3rd, when Justin was sentenced to the maximum prison time allowable under federal sentencing guidelines.

Justin violated the first code of conduct for ALF warriors when captured -- never cooperate with the enemy against

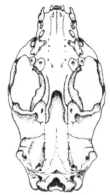

illustration of mink skull

fellow activists. Another lesson once again painfully learned by Justin is that the U.S. Government is an immoral and unethical oppressor that historically has broken any and all promises in order to further its own objectives. Our credo must remain that when asked to incriminate our comrades, we will never negotiate with government terrorists and hostage takers.

Another key mistake was that Justin, under the advice of his lawyers, asked that his name be removed from prisoner lists and that no activists write to him in the hopes that disassociation would improve his odds at sentencing. By doing that, Justin instead cut himself off from the immense international support our movement has for direct action prisoners. Instead of receiving large amounts of mail that improve one's psychological strength and well-being, Justin faced his opponents alone and was deceived by the government's false promises.

Rather than direct vindictive energy towards Justin, we must focus on the need to strengthen the resiliency of our warriors so they can endure the intimidation faced once captured. It helps no one, least of all the oppressed animal nations, to allow ourselves to harbor the kind of anger and hatred we are supposed to be against. Having seen for himself that nothing can be gained by cooperating with the U.S. Government, Justin has months to think about his mistakes.

Don't get me wrong. As the subject of past grand jury investigations I know what it's like to have former friends testify against you. But rather than having hatred for those responsible, I instead choose to recognize that some of us in the animal liberation community do not have the strength one needs to remain unbroken in prison or close-mouthed in front of grand jury interrogators.

Because of that, it's vital to remind direct action warriors that if you can't do the time, don't do the crime. You help no one if you can only carry out actions but cannot remain tight-lipped about them. ALF actions are about more than getting the animals out and destroying the tools of their torture; ALF actions require warriors to be ready to be treated like violent criminals in the courtrooms of the earth and animals' destroyers. We must be prepared to go to prison for years rather than utter a word about our still free fighting comrades.

In the Ellerman brothers' case in Utah and now with Justin, we've seen the damage down when warriors break and testify against each other. And ironically, it's those who cooperate who end up in prison for years, not those they testify against. An old friend once told me, "...nobody talks, and everybody walks..."

Now we must exercise some damage control and build support for Peter Young who faces an uphill battle when and if he's captured. Justin's testimony doesn't help, but it may not be enough to convict Peter as the 1998 Utah ALF case illustrated.

We must also organize and raise awareness and funds to aid Josh Harper and Andy Stepanian. Josh is facing imprisonment for contempt while Andy's sentencing for fur shop actions in New York should have passed by print time. Both of these brave warriors are deeply committed to the causes of freedom, but their strength cannot be a substitute for the very real support they need from us.

And while the Fur Information Council touts Justin's conviction as a victory and the first successful application of the Animal Enterprise Protection Act, it's encouraging to see that despite earlier threats, a multi-state ALF campaign that resulted in the release of over 6,000 mink and hundreds of thousands of dollars in financial loss to fur farmers netted Justin only 24 months and not the ten years or more some feared under this draconian legislation.

It remains the obligation of every ALF warrior: Be prepared to accept the negative and unpleasant ramifications of your actions. Be ready to do your time bravely and positively rather than compromise your comrades and the larger struggle with your inability to do so. In addition, a movement that engages in illegal tactics must ensure that its participants have total support before, during and after their sacrifice for the earth and her animal nations. Only then will cooperation with all our oppressors no longer be an option.

Setting Free the Prisoners

The Ecological Consequences of Releasing Mink

This article comes from the Nov/Dec 2003 issue of the Earth First Journal. Rod wrote it in response for the often stated misconception that releasing mink from fur farms creates some sort of ecological disaster.

artwork by Jerico

*F*ifty million years ago, mustelids stalked their prey with the same streamlined body and pointed head that their descendants, the American mink, hunt with today. Indeed, fossil records suggest that today's water-savvy mink have changed little from their forest-dwelling ancestors. Of the 15 naturally occurring subspecies of mink in North America, six are being selectively bred in captivity. The genetic integrity of these mink is threatened by fur farms who are domesticating the species for commercial exploitation.

On August 25, the Animal Liberation Front (ALF) released 10,000 mink from the Roesler Brothers Fur Farm in Snohomish County, Washington. This action marked the 57th such raid since the ALF began opening fur farm cages in North America in 1995. The tactic is not new, however, with the ALF having first introduced this strategy against the fur trade in the UK in the 1980s.

Since farmers began breeding mink in the early 1920s, only the color, length and quality of the animals' fur has been affected. Outside of these factors, the mink being raised on the 400 mink farms in the US are genetically identical to their wild cousins. The fact that fur-farm mink so readily adapt to feral life indicates that the attempted domestication has so far had a negligible effect on their race.

Mass mink releases have presented a sometimes difficult question for environmentalists who oppose the domestication of native wildlife but fear the impact that large numbers of mink would have on the surrounding environment. According to Nigel Dunstone in his thoroughly researched book, *The Mink*, "While the mink is no model of benevolence, many years of research in the field have revealed no evidence of the ecological disasters so often predicted."

At the 1991 Seattle Fur Exchange auctions, I interviewed numerous mink farmers, none of whom questioned the potential survivability of farm-raised mink in the wild. Most states require that mink farms have a perimeter fence surrounding mink barns to prevent escapes.

Whether mink can survive is less of a question than what ecological impacts such introductions have on native wildlife, especially fish, ground-nesting birds and small mammals. In England, research on the effects of feral mink on salmonid stocks revealed that the mink did little more than impact surplus populations of smaller fish.

Meanwhile, sea bird nesting colonies can be especially vulnerable to feral mink. On islands off the coasts of Scotland, Sweden, Finland, Iceland and Norway, sea birds have been heavily preyed upon by feral mink, sometimes forcing the birds to nest on islands further offshore. In the US, an entire colony of spotted sandpipers was wiped out by marauding mink. Yet, the majority of animals preyed upon by feral mink remain abundant, including rabbits and rats.

Nonetheless, even 100 hungry and fierce small predators can be capable of wrecking havoc on domestic and wild animals. In Snohomish County, less than a mile from the Roesler Brothers farm, escaping mink killed chickens and other animals. One neighboring farmer lost 29 exotic birds to mink attacks.

In times of low prey availability, mink have been known to kill beyond their immediate needs in order to stockpile prey for future consumption. Understandably, any artificial populations of small animals such as ducks or chickens are vulnerable to feral mink predation. As biocentrists, this should be the last reason to oppose the return of captive mink to their rightful home in the wild.

On average, only 30 percent of the mink released during fur farm raids actually escape into the surrounding environment. In Washington, where there have been seven mass releases since 1996, that impact is unnoticeable as these normally shy and solitary animals quickly distribute themselves over a large area.

Once wild, mink regulate their numbers according to the availability of suitable habitat and prey. According to Dunstone's research, a mink's intolerance of other mink will ensure a low population density. Aggressiveness toward their own kind make mink their own number one predator.

Any ethical debate on the merits of causing such a predator-prey reaction must first be leveled against the fur farm industry itself. It is solely responsible for sustaining large concentrations of predators in cramped and unnatural conditions. The attempted domestication of mink is fraught with problems ranging from physical neurosis in the form of self-mutilation to diseases unknown to wild mink.

The often rural and mountainous regions where mink farms are located are far from pristine, untrammeled wilderness. These areas are affected by threats much greater than those posed by released mink, such as habitat destruction, water diversion and pollution.

In North America, no biological evidence has been documented or published revealing long-term negative ecological impacts from the ALF's mink releases. The ALF has always favored simple release as a tool of economic sabotage and the quickest avenue toward animal liberation. The financial impact such actions have on fur farms is monumental. And while offering an often slim chance for permanent freedom, the ALF's actions are nonetheless offering mink a chance—one arguably better than the animals' certain death. The vilification of mink as a significant predator of native fauna and domestic stock, or as a competitor with native carnivores, is largely without foundation.

Following numerous ALF raids, released mink have been killed by automobiles, and some animals have suffered fur damage from fights with other mink. In Snohomish County, recaptured mink are killing each other.

"Mink are fine when littermates are caged together, but when they're not, they're quite vicious and do eat each other. That's what we're battling," says a Roesler Brothers fur farmer.

While unfortunate, the result is still to further deny income to mink farmers. At the Roesler Brothers Fur Farm, the cost of the ALF's August raid was an estimated $500,000. While an ethical dilemma for some, fur farmers and liberators alike acknowledge the financial impact the action carries to the stability of a mink farm.

Still, there comes a responsibility with the mass release of mink. The targeted area for mink releases should be carefully researched, and raids should be carried out in consideration of threatened or endangered wildlife in the surrounding ecosystem. The single most effective solution remains the permanent closure of all mink farms and the ecologically responsible rehabilitation and release of their native prisoners.

We live in a time where there are no easy or ethical answers to the problems posed by exotic non native species, Euro-American *Homo sapiens* being at the top of the list. As biocentrists, we must balance our idealism with pragmatism. With farm-raised mink, the answers come easily. Earth First! and other deep ecologists should oppose the attempted domestication of the American mink by the fur industry before this native predator becomes yet another human-dependent species that exists solely for our commercial exploitation. In this regard, the ALF stands as the only organization actively pursuing this goal.

Book One:

Strong Hearts

In yourselves you must find heroes

artwork by Jerico

STRONG HEARTS
INTRO

*W*elcome to Strong Hearts #1! For those of you whom I have yet to have the pleasure of meeting, this should let you understand a bit about the thoughts and beliefs that have led me down this winding road with the present rest stop in prison.

Why my own zine? Well, when I first entered prison about a year ago I was feeling a bit isolated from all I love. The earth, her animal people, crystal rivers, campfires and my beloved friends, family and community members all were taken from me when I became known to the US government as Prisoner 03895-000. Now, as I live largely by my connections with the outside world through letters, books, newsletters and zines I want to give something back to all the beautiful people who have supported me on the path of resistance to the dark forces that plague our planet. Some of you have been friends since my early years with Sea Shepherd and Earth First! and others since my return to my homeland here in Arizona. Some of you I know only by your brilliant letters that keep my heart alive when others would attempt to break it by imprisoning me. Anyway, I'm drifting. This zine is the product of thoughts and feelings that sometimes make me cry and other times leave me feeling like that happiest man on the earth, even in here.

The animals I write about are those that I believe have yet to be conquered by Manifest Destiny, the people I write of are those I believe have accepted our responsibility to defend our earth, animals and people from the forces who are destroying all creation. In some small way I hope this zine helps remind you that the battle is far from over, and far from lost. It's up to every one of us to do our part to ensure that future generations of humans and other animals are able to breathe fresh air, drink clean water, eat good food and continue the dance that we call life. With that I leave you now to the freedom of your own thoughts. May the creator bless each and every one of us, the Children of Earth.

RAID ON REYKJAVIł

*O*n my very first trip at sea and aboard the *Sea Shepherd* in 1985, we were crossing the North Atlantic from Halifax, Nova Scotia to the Danish Faeroe Islands where we were to interfere with the annual pilot whale slaughter there. Along the way we stopped to refuel in Reykjavik, Iceland, home of the country's only whaling fleet. As soon as we docked police patrols were set up around our ship and the whalers. Also, divers were sent down daily to check the whaling ships for mines we might have placed on their hulls at night. All pretty flattering stuff, really.

Meanwhile, Greenpeace had their ship, the Sirius, there as well and jealousy arose as their visit had not merited such attention. They joined with the Icelanders and called us terrorists for sinking whaling ships, and banned our crew from visiting their ship. Journalists on board complained to us that while they were in port Greenpeace had watched passively and did nothing as the whaling ships went to sea to kill whales. As long as Sea Shepherd was in town, the whalers refused to go to sea. Captain Paul Watson told them we were on our way to the Faeroe Islands; but if Iceland refused to abide by the international moratorium on commercial whaling, which would take effect the following summer, we would be back.

One day while in port, I walked to the part of the harbor where the whaling ships were and watched the police watch me and told myself, "I bet that if we were not here, there would be no police guard on the whalers..." Besides the cops, there was only one watchman onboard for all four whalers. I buried that information in the back of my mind where I keep all my other little schemes to save the earth and went back to the Sea Shepherd.

A year later, and I was onboard the Sea Shepherd again: this time in Malmo, Sweden for the International Whaling Commission (IWC) conference. There the big news was that Iceland was refusing to cease their whaling operations, despite the worldwide moratorium to assess whale populations. And every other whaling nation in the world was watching to see what the member nations would do since the IWC lacked any enforcement body, save individual member nations' economic power in the form of sanctions. Captain Watson repeated his warning to Iceland to abide by the moratorium or face enforcement of the moratorium by the Sea Shepherd.

Later, the Sea Shepherd would be the first and only non-governmental observer to be banned from the IWC for having done just that. That summer we returned to the Faeroe Islands to successfully interfere with the pilot whale slaughter again. I got beat up, arrested and jailed by the police for the first time, and after my release rejoined the Sea Shepherd where we returned to have a running battle with the Faroese Patrol Vessel, the Olivar Hagli.

It was amazing. They were trying to board our vessel at sea, lobbing tear gas canisters onboard, but we threw every one back at them and I got to shoot flares and a firehose at the same Faroese cop who had beaten and arrested me. Very empowering stuff, but that's another story. In that battle, one brave crew member shined bright, the young Cornish engineer David Howitt who kept the Sea Shepherd rolling by pushing our engines to the max despite the engine room being 120 degrees and full of tear gas. Had we lost speed or stopped, we not only would have lost the ship, but we'd have probably gotten our asses kicked big-time by the Faroese and gone to jail for a very long time.

But we didn't and sailed for Bristol, England. Now that our summer campaign was over, my thoughts shifted back to Iceland's whaling industry. News reports stated that Icelandic whalers had filled a self-imposed quota of 80 sei whales and 40 fin— both endangered species. Late one night after our watches, I approached David, who by now was a good friend. We sat on piles of ships' lines in the rope locker and shared a smoke. Finally, I told him my idea of trying to infiltrate Iceland with the sole purpose of causing maximum economic sabotage to their whaling industry. David agreed that it seemed an appropriate action against a whaling nation that was flagrantly violating the IWC ban on whaling. It was decided. We would take action on behalf of the last great whale nations.

Next, I approached Paul and told him of our plan. As we gently sailed the warm summer sea, we quietly talked of the plan as if we were discussing something as simple as tides and currents, not something that if there was failure could land David and me in prison for years. Paul gave us his blessing and with that our mission became a reality. Looking back on that day, it is easy to understand why I have such great respect and admiration for Paul Watson. Here I was, a 20 year-old kid telling him how I and a 23 year-old British hunt saboteur planned to carry out a major covert operation against an island nation that had already been threatened with the very same action. We were not Green Berets or Navy Seals, yet Paul never once told us he doubted our success. He just asked us what we needed, and by not questioning our abilities gave us the vote of self-confidence we needed to believe we could be successful.

In late July, David and I signed off the crew of the Sea Shepherd, telling others we were of on a tour of Europe. No suspicion was raised except by Nick Taylor, our British friend who had fought the police alongside me and shared a Faroese jail cell with me too. Nick could not believe we were off to do something so frivolous, and we could tell he was deeply disappointed in us. Later, before our departure to Reykjavik, we would return to the Sea Shepherd and confess to Nick our real intentions. We knew it had hurt him that we were leaving him alone to care for the Sea Shepherd through the long English winter. Nick was pleased, and the last words he ever spoke to me were, "It must be great doing something you really believe in…" A few month later, Nick committed suicide after he began to slip back into a life of drug abuse.

David and I spent the whole summer of 1986 working to raise the money for our mission. I waited tables in a nightclub in London's Chelsea district during the nights and refinished antiques on Kings Road during the day. David went to southern England where he picked hops. Every few weeks we would meet to discuss our plans and go over intelligence we had gathered on Iceland. When our work was complete, we would make a batch of paint-filled light bulbs and ride out on our bikes to redecorate London fur shops. Finally, the day arrived when we rode the London Underground subway to Heathrow Airport to catch our IcelandAir flight to Reykjavik. As we rode to the airport, I removed a patch from my jacket that read "Save the Whales, Save the Earth" with a picture of a fin whale. All we carried with us was our cameras, clothes and raingear, underwater flashlights, knives and a couple maps. All the tools necessary for my action would be acquired in Iceland.

When we arrived in October only the hardcore tourists were still around. We got beds in the local youth hostel. One of our first tasks was to buy a pair of bolt cutters and a large adjustable wrench from a local hardware store. We wanted as much time as possible between the purchase of our tools and the action, in case someone might remember the purchase. On one of our first nights in the capital city of Reykjavik we snuck out of the hostel late at night and snuck to a scrap yard from where we could view the four 175-foot Icelandic ships that comprised the nation's entire whaling fleet. Hvalur (whaling ships) 5, 6, 7 and 8 bobbed in the harbor, tied alongside each other like the Four Riders of the Apocalypse waiting to unleash their evil on the natural world. The ships' superstructures were painted white, with the bridge windows and portholes dark and imposing, resembling the eye sockets of a skull.

Needless to say, we were a little intimidated. The reality of what was so simple to discuss in England, but what was staring at us in the face in the freezing fall weather of a Reykjavik night, was more than a little daunting. But we knew it would not be easy, so we began a series of late night observations of the harbor. Within two weeks of surveillance a definite routine began to emerge. Every Friday night, a watchman would relieve the day watch carrying with him two bottles of Brenivin, a strong Icelandic vodka. No activity could be seen on three of the ships, the watchman staying on the fourth ship, the one furthest from the dock; a weekend night emerged as the best night for action.

In Reykjavik, we saw photos from the whaling station which was 45 miles from town. Tours were offered for the station, so David and I hitchhiked to the desolate station and dropped off near the entrance. As we approached, not a soul was visible. The whaling season was over, and with it the demand for tours. David and I began to walk throughout the premises in broad daylight, gazing through windows at offices, machinery and workshops. It quickly became evident to both of us that we might be able to strike the whaling station also. We knew we would only have one shot at the Icelandic whaling industry, and any risk to ourselves did not matter— already we felt the chances were high we would not get off the island once our sabotage was discovered.

Next, our intelligence gathering revealed that Iceland was only allowed to export 49% of the whale meat of Japan and that the majority would have to be for local consumption. Yet the supermarkets offered very little. Whale meat was no longer a staple of the Icelandic diet. We began the search for the Whalemeat Mountain, as newspapers called it, and this meant me taking a job as a meat packer in the packing plant that packaged whale meat. The job was easy to get as there is virtually no unemployment in Iceland and unattractive jobs like meat-packing are often given to foreigners.

David and I had to keep up our image of adventurers and travelers so we socialized with Swedish, German and Irish tourists. We would frequent the café overlooking the harbor where, while socializing and drinking coffee, we could keep an eye on the whaling ships. Then one day at work there was an immigration sweep and my boss was forced to fire me; but what really worried me was the background check they might run on me. Based on my actions and arrest in the Faroes I had been issued an expulsion from the whole of Scandinavia, including Iceland. I had violated that order by not only returning to the Faroes but also by fighting off the police as they tried to board our vessel. If the Icelandic authorities discovered I was wanted in the Faroes not only would our mission be revealed by the tools and photos in our belongings, but also I might be extradited to Denmark.

My boss was apologetic and even advanced me some money from his own wallet. Meanwhile, David and I decided that we must either abort our mission and flee the country immediately, or stay and try to carry out the action. We chose the latter. We had been in Iceland for almost a month now and felt familiar with the habits of the watchmen aboard the whaling ships and confident we could also strike the whaling station. We also had visited a small zoo outside of Reykjavik which housed a few native animals, including one Orca whale that had been captured recently and was to be sold to an aquarium. David and I looked at each other trying to figure how the hell we could get that whale out of its tank and into the ocean just a hundred yards away, but here we were forced to realize the bounds of our limitations. Still, should time allow, it was decided that after striking the whaling station and the whaling ships we would hit the zoo and release as many native animals as possible.

Iceland in November was not a country that expected (not even remembered) the threats of militant anti-whaling organizations. Just as I had expected in the summer visit of 1985, without our visible presence only one watchman was aboard all four ships. It was the off season and the crews were ashore, with work on the ships restricted to daylight hours. The week of our planned attack, the whaling ships were taken into drydock. One by one, they were pulled out of the water for repairs and cleaning, which is a major operation. David and I had planned on attempting to sink all three ships minus the one that housed the watchman. Now we were forced to sacrifice this target. Our money was running low and the fear of being discovered still haunted us. Maybe we were already under surveillance ourselves and the police were waiting for us to act before they could legitimately arrest us?

David and I had already read up on the Icelandic penal system and learned that the longest sentence given to any crime was eleven years. From that day on the jokes never stopped about how good we might become at building Icelandic sidewalks. Finally, surrendering our fate to the whale spirits, we decided to act. We chose the night of November 7th for our attack of vengeance. We said goodbye to our European friends and told them David and I were going to rent a car for our last day to do a little sightseeing.

We drove to the airport on the morning of the 7th to pre-check our luggage for the 6 a.m. flight out of the country the following morning. It was to Luxemburg, but we did not care where it went as long as it was not Scandinavia. Next we drove to Iceland's only vegetarian restaurant for what might be our last supper. We had been saving our money for this last luxury, but found the restaurant closed. Not to be disappointed, we bought food from a supermarket and drove to a clearing above the whaling station to eat our meal and await the early winter darkness. While eating we listened to the car radio and after our meal discovered we had drained the battery dead. Here our mission might have been ended had not a van-load of Icelandic youth, who were probably employed by the whaling station, come to our rescue. They towed our car until we could jump start it and then we waved goodbye and drove to our prearranged hiding place for the car as night was fast approaching.

A rainstorm began to fall adding a brilliant cover as David and I pulled on our dark raingear, gloves and ski-masks and strapped on fanny-packs with flashlights and tools. I then placed the car keys on the top of the rear tire and we began the long walk to the whaling station in complete darkness, bending into the wind and increasing rain. As we approached the whaling station we were surprised by the sight and sound of a front end excavator that was digging a trench at the station. We dropped to the ground and spent the next hour lying in the freezing rain until the workman and his machine headed off to the local town. As the lights of the machine disappeared, we leaped into action.

After this task we found the computer control room that kept the entire station's machinery fully automated. We smashed the computer panels until sparks flew and LEDs flashed and the beautiful music of machines dying all around us could be heard. There was no time to waste, so we moved next to the ships' store where spare parts for the four whaling ships were kept. Taking the most expensive pieces, we walked to the edge of the docks and tossed them into the waters. We finally reached the offices where record books detailing the illegal catches were confiscated and cyanic acid was poured through the building. Windows were smashed and anything that looked expensive met the business end of our wrenches and bolt cutters.

Our first task was the sabotage of the six huge diesel generators that provided power for the station. David and I were both experienced diesel engineers and we knew what was good for the engine and what was bad. Before long we were stripping off our outer clothing and sweating profusely from our handiwork. Next, we moved onto the centrifuges that processed whale blubber into a high grade lubricating oil that was used in missiles. Smashing the delicate gear, we next located what we could not find in the meat packing plant: the Whalemeat Mountain. Housed in huge refrigeration units beneath the station, David had attempted to move the many crates of whale meat near the slipway where whales were dragged up for processing, but the forklift he drove ran out of gas. We were forced to wedge open the refrigeration units and then sabotage the units themselves, so that hopefully the meat would thaw and spoil.

Watching World News a few days later, we would hear the foreman of the station recounting with shock how it appeared that the whole whaling station had been the target of an air raid. We could have spent all night sabotaging the station but the ships were waiting so David and I signaled a retreat and returned, tired and sweating, to our car. Once there I experienced a frantic moment as I reached for the keys on the tire and found them not there. The high winds had been so strong as to blow them some feet away, where I found them with my flashlight. Covered now in grease and drenched in sweat, we drove back to Reykjavik. The weather made the roads treacherous and often the car would start to slide when it hit ice.

I am convinced that many of my premature grey hairs were earned that night. An hour later we reached the Reykjavik Harbor, where three ships lay bobbing in the water, the fourth in drydock. Resting, David and I ate some quick energy food and stashed our confiscated record books from the whaling station in the backseat. Taking a deep breath, we opened our car doors and stepped back into the pounding rainstorm that made our ski-masks and rain gear a necessity, not just a disguise. With hands in our pockets like two old fishermen, we walked down the dead-end dock towards Hvalur 5, 6 and 7.

The tides in the harbor were such as so we were level with the ship decks, so to board all we had to do was hop the few feet from the dock to the steel plated decks. Moving quickly to Hvalur 5, David pulled out our bolt cutters and cut the hasp on the lock that shut the engine room hatch. Moving into the fully lit engine rooms, David searched the ship for any sleeping watchmen while I moved into the engine room and began lifting deck plates, looking for the saltwater cooling valve that regulated sea water, which cooled the ships' engines at sea. By the time I found it David had returned to announce that the ship was indeed empty. We began to wrestle off the sixteen or more nuts that held the valve cover in place and when most were removed water began to shoot out from the bolt holes. I tasted it and it was salty. When the cover was fully removed, the ocean water would flood first the engine room and then the rest of the ships compartments, dragging it to a watery grave in Reykjavik's deep harbor. Leaving the cover partially removed, we moved to Hvalur 6, where, repeating the process, we quickly located and began to remove that ship's salt water cooling valve.

Finally, with all the nuts and bolts removed, we took a pry bar to the valve and with a little persuasion the valve popped free, releasing a flood of seawater that drenched both David and I. Quickly returning to Hvalur 5, we removed the last of that ship's valve cover bolts and again the ocean began to rush in. Now it was time to execute our escape. The whaling station had been demolished and two 175-foot whaling ships were sinking. It was just before five in the morning and the airport was about and hour away. Walking away from the two sinking ships we tossed our tools into the icy waters and pulled our ski-masks off just as we reached the car. Hopping into the driver seat, I started the car and pulled onto the road and not two minutes later was pulled over by a Reykjavik cop car.

My first thought was, "No, they can't be that good, they couldn't have been watching us all this time…" Still, there we were: two ships quickly sinking, minutes ticking away before our flight to freedom would lift off, maybe leaving us fine-tuning our masonry skills in the local prison for the next eleven years, and a police officer walking up to my window with David and I soaked in sea water with grease from the engines all over our clothes. The officer asked me to get into his car. Looking at David, who sat with eyes forward, I got out of the car and got into the backseat of the police cruiser. The officers ignored me and spoke to each other in Icelandic before finally turning around and asking me in plain English, "Have you drunken any alcohol tonight?" Almost laughing, I said, "No, I don't even drink!" which was a lie and then the cop asked to smell my breath. So, I breathed on him and he wished me a safe trip to the airport, knowing that is where we were headed because of the early morning departure.

That police officer is probably still cursing himself after having the nation's only saboteur since the Second World War in his car and then letting him go. Returning to the car, David told me he had almost bolted but thought it best he waited another moment for some signal from me. The zoo liberation was now out of the question as we sped towards the airport to catch our 6 a.m. flight. Pulling into the airport, we grabbed our daypacks and quickly changed our clothes, dumping the grease covered ones in the airport garbage can. We next went through Icelandic Customs without any incident and checked in and grabbed our boarding passes. The polite ticket agent told us the flight was delayed due to the harsh weather. The words were the worst we wanted to hear and David and I spent the next 30 minutes staring at the clock, imagining the chaos erupting at the Reykjavik harbor just about now. Finally, our flight was called and we quickly boarded, still not feeling safe until we landed in Luxemburg.

Hours later as the plane landed, David and I gazed out the window half expecting to see Interpol agents waiting for our arrival. They were not. We collected our luggage and walked out of the airport after making an anonymous call to Sea Shepherd offices in the UK saying only, "we got the station and two are on the bottom..." We hitchhiked to Belgium where we caught a ferry to England and then a bus to London. Getting off the bus, now 36 hours after our action, I walked to a news agent and picked up a copy of the morning paper. A story on the front page said only, "SABOTEURS SINK WHALERS, photos page six..." flipping to the page I saw one of the most beautiful sights in the world. There was Hvalur 5 and 6 resting gently on the bottom of the Reykjavik harbor, only their skeletal superstructures peeking above the waves. Paul Watson was quoted as accepting responsibility for the attack, which he said was an enforcement action of the IWC's moratorium on commercial whaling that Iceland had violated. David and I embraced in the streets, laughing with the elation that only a realized dream can bring.

The next few weeks saw David go into hiding in the Mediterranean, not knowing Britain's response to his actions, while I flew back Stateside to join Paul in a press conference in Cleveland Amory's office at the Fund for Animals to accept personal responsibility for the raid. The confiscated record books would prove that Iceland had cheated with its own imposed quota, having shipped more than the maximum 49% whale meat catch to Japan. A special meeting of the Icelandic Congress was held to address the act of sabotage and the called for extradition of those responsible. Paul could not agree more and said it would give the Sea Shepherd the opportunity to put Iceland on trial and also in the spotlight of international media, where their pirate whaling operations could be exposed. Iceland never pressed charges against me or David. Though Hvalur 5 and 6 were finally resurfaced, the saltwater submersion had destroyed all the engines, electrical and navigational equipment. To this day, neither ship has killed a single whale and the harpoons are silenced in Iceland...for now.

REHABILITATION AND REINTRODUCTION OF TWO LYNX

*T*he first Canadian Lynx I ever saw was, sadly enough, in a cage. Another native American animal whose contact with humans is on our own terms and not theirs. After crawling through knee-high grass with Montana's Mission Mountain Wilderness behind us, a friend and I could lift our binoculars and see the rows of cages on the Fraser Fur Ranch in Ronan. Before us lay hundreds of imprisoned bobcats and lynx and thousands of mink. Later I would learn that though the mink were some sixty generations out of the wild, the bobcats and lynx were only one- to three-generations out of the wild and some were actually captured in the nearby mountains. The victims of steel-jaw leg-hold traps that had survived the trauma only to be hogtied and brought down to the fur farm from their wilderness home. Now they were destined to spend their entire lives pacing the confines of their four-foot square wire cage, gazing at the mountain wilderness that once was their domain.

Canadian Lynx have only been called "Canadian" since the time they were slowly pushed out of their former range in the United States. Though isolated pockets of wild lynx populations still exist in the US, the largest numbers now reside in Canada. In Montana, despite depleted numbers, there is still a trapping season for lynx. Further west, in the Cascade mountain chain, lynx not long ago roamed as far south as Central Oregon. Logging has since been responsible for the destruction of large, undisturbed forests that the solitary lynx require for their survival. Forced into the Northern Cascades of Eastern Washington, lynx are making what might be their last stand here in the Okanaga forests, where their last habitat is once again under the blade of the chainsaw.

So it was with great sadness that my first encounter with this noble animal relation was as yet another prisoner of the war on nature that was reduced to the physical worth that humans saw in our wild relations. For the Lynx Nation, this meant intensive confinement in cages like those on Fraser Fur Ranch where they were forced to breed offspring that would be raised until their beautiful fur reached its prime at which point they would be shot in the head and have their belly fur stripped from their bodies to provide luxurious fur coats for aristocrats in far off lands.

The location of Fraser Fur Ranch had been given to us by the friendly biologist at the local Montana Game, Wildlife and Parks office in Kalispell where we inquired about fur farms and where we might purchase breeding stock for our own future farm, a cover for our investigations of fur farming. Later, we would visit the small ranch of the MGWP biologist who himself raised mink for their fur. Besides his few hundred mink, the biologist also had four bobcats and two lynx that he had acquired from the Fraser Ranch to attempt to breed his own.

When I first approached the lynx in their small cages it was easy to see that they were very much still wild. Low growls rolled from their throats and they pushed themselves as far as possible away from us in their exposed cages. I was ashamed to see such a regal beast reduced to such a shameful purpose. Lynx, I knew, were believed to be supernatural beings by many of the Northern Nations of indigenous peoples who came into contact with them. Their ghost-like appearance and ability to walk on the fresh fallen snow without sinking in gave them the prestige that only humans living in harmony and close to the earth could understand. Eventually our friendship with the fur farmer biologist grew to the point that we would strike a deal to buy out his small farm after having witnessed and documented the neck breaking of his mink. Though our interest was primarily in the mink, and the fur farmers deal offered to us included only his mink, we responded that we wanted to buy out his complete fur farm, lynx and bobcats included. After the grisly neck breaking episode, my friend and I were sick to our stomachs that we had not done more to spare the animals' lives. So it was decided that we would buy out the remaining animals and rehabilitate and release them all. Our fur farmer friend set a price, and a week later we were back in Montana with the cash and U-haul truck necessary to relocate the animals.

None of us had a clue how we were going to go about the massive project of rehabilitating the mink, bobcats and lynx, but we made the promise to the animals that we would, and so began an experience that would change our lives forever. Not having any land of my own to take the animals to, I had called on an old Sea Shepherd friend who had experience with wildlife rehabilitation work.

I told her that I had just bought sixty mink, four bobcats and two lynx and had no place to take them; would she be interested in helping us to return them to the wild? And like the true friend she is, she responded immediately with a definite yes. In mid-December 1990, we loaded all the animals into a 26-foot long truck and drove west to the Olympic Peninsula. A recent snow storm had left the highways treacherous, and as we headed west I could not help but worry about our precious cargo should we slide off the road like so many other cars around us. We drove throughout the night, and early the next morning arrived at what we all would soon be calling "The Sanctuary."

My dear friend David Howitt and I spent one of the best Christmas' ever in my life working in the freezing cold, building larger pens for the bobcats and lynx. Our finances were nil, and I was forced to beg and borrow to provide for the animals; the stealing would come later. My task was to recruit more people to help with the large task, and friends from Oregon quickly filled the bill.

Before long, five of the best friends I've ever had in my life were working days and nights to try and guarantee freedom for these former fur farm prisoners. At this stage in the game I was still hoping Friends of Animals, who had sponsored the fur farm investigation, would help us achieve our goals. They were totally non-supportive and even resentful that we had entered into such a project without their approval. Finally they offered to take the animals off our hands and ship them all to a sanctuary in Texas where they would live out their lives in cages.

Our sanctuary crew held an impromptu meeting and I told them the news. None of us were happy about the offer. We all shared the same feeling. We had pledged ourselves to these few survivors of the fur industry's war on wildlife not to find them a life in a cage, but a shot at freedom. We discussed our alternatives. I told everyone that I was not about to give these animals over to a group who seemed more concerned with capitalizing off of animals' suffering than saving real lives. We had spent a year risking our own necks sneaking onto fur farms to obtain the evidence all of us in the movement wanted, but where FoA was happy with the photos and videos we had, it was up to us alone to give them true freedom. We decided to refuse FoA's offer.

We had no money, yet we agreed to carry out the rehabilitation on our own. Over the next six months it was not unusual to see our volunteers go without a meal so that the animals would have enough to eat. The sanctuary crew were tireless, working seven days a week in freezing wether without complaint. Never have I witnessed a more committed group of activists determined to deliver our goal of these animals' liberation.

By February it was plain to see that the lynx would be the easiest to rehabilitate. After all, they were still very wild and fearful of human beings. It was time to move the lynx to larger enclosures where they could touch the earth and exercise their muscles for the hardships of the wild. The problem was that we did not have the money to purchase the chain-link fence needed to build the pens.

The frustration of our poverty had hampered us before, but had yet to stop us. We were determined to give the cats what they deserved, and who better to make an "involuntary donation" than the State of Washington, who sanctioned fur farming and hunting and trapping of other fur-bearers. Late one night we piled into the sanctuary van and raided a fenced lot, taking with us the fencing material needed to build two 26-foot square enclosures.

Getting back to work, we erected the pens around naturally vegetated areas where the cats could begin their rehabilitation. The lynx were housed separately; we did not want the female to become pregnant and further burden herself during her first season back in the wild. Next, we introduced a natural diet. A lynx's diet consists almost exclusively of snowshoe hares, whose population swings in a ten-year cycle, thereby influencing the lynx populations. We did some research and discovered that 1991 was a peak year, and the lynx moved one step closer to freedom.

Soon we were feeding the lynx only live rabbits, and once they had proven their proficiency in killing their prey, we decided to start scoping-out release sites. The lynx had had over two months in their large pens, where they were completely isolated from all human view. Slowly, we had watched their wild spirits reawaken and we knew the time had come to return these prisoners to their rightful homes. We were tempted to release the lynx in an area where lynx had been wiped out, hoping that they would breed and replenish the area. But our research revealed that two animals were far too few to begin the reintroduction of a species, so our search shifted to a habitat already inhabited by lynx, no matter how few. Taking a map of known lynx range, we circled the largest roadless area and drew an X on the center area.

Next we drove as close as we could to the area, and as we arrived at night the first thing we saw were snowshoe hares running away from our car. The road leading to the trailhead we would need to carry the lynx to had been closed by a major washout by the nearby river.

Also, many trees had fallen over the road and when we inquired at the local US Forest Service office about when the road would be cleared, we were told that budget cuts prevented them from clearing the road for at least two years. Again, the lynx made light steps closer to freedom.

Returning to the sanctuary with the good news, we next enlisted the help of a Blackfoot Medicine Woman from the area where the lynx descended from. Administering a blessing to the animals, we watched in amazement as she freely moved amongst the lynx in their pens, smudging them with sweetgrass and sage. The animals seemed to be intrigued by the woman, watching attentively her every movement. The Medicine Woman instructed us on how we should smudge each animal again before their release and, this having been done, each animal would find its path back to the wilderness world.

By this time I had known these lynx personally for over ten months. Slowly I had began to see in them the spirit that at times I felt they could see right through me to my innermost hidden feelings and fears. I was humbled in their presence. In their cages on the fur farm in Montana they appeared to be fallen angels captured by the cruel callousness of Man. Now they appeared to be returning to their power. Their regalness returned and it became frightfully easy to understand why they were believed to be supernatural. They are. In the spring snowmelt of 1991, we began to map out our release strategy. Reintroducing captive-bred native wildlife was illegal. Any liberation would have to be conducted covertly or else the lynx might fall into the bloody hands of the wildlife agencies that sanction the killing for sport and profit of the lynx's wild brethren.

The night arrived when four chosen liberators were gathered together at the sanctuary for the long journey to freedom. Already the lynx's feeding had been supplemented with roadkilled rabbits in preparation for their release. A livetrap was borrowed from the local humane society to transfer the lynx from their pens to two separate boxes outfitted with handles to facilitate carrying by two people. The boxes were completely covered with a sliding door on one end.

Once in the boxes, the lynx were loaded into the back of a truck, and a guide car led our procession away from the sanctuary to the ferry terminal where we would cross to Kingston, and then onto the mountains. When we arrived at the ferry terminal we discovered we had missed the last ferry and were forced to drive south to a ferry terminal that would place us right in downtown Seattle. Without any reasonable alternative, we boarded the ferry and had a meeting to discuss our escape from Seattle with two live lynx.

The three liberators in the guide car were instructed to follow us a few car lengths behind, and should the unfortunate situation present itself that we were pulled over by the police, the guide car was to serve as a decoy by speeding ahead to divert the police's attention. It was a crazy idea, but we refused to even consider allowing the lynx to fall into the hands of the State. We deboarded the ferry and drove down the dark city streets of Seattle trying to pretend that we did not have two adult lynx in the back of our pick-up truck.

With the escape from Seattle complete, we began the long drive north towards the desolate wilderness where only lynx belonged. We left behind the freeways, and then the small rural towns and soon began our ascent into the mountainous area that we had previously scouted. The scent of pine and cedar greeted our noses, and I began to daydream about what must be going through the lynx's minds and hearts about now.

Back at the sanctuary I had learned that, like their domestic counterparts, the lynx–I believed–had the ability to almost telepathically sense the thoughts and feelings of humans around them. It had began as an experiment: to fill my mind with images, not words, that the lynx could understand whenever I was forced to be around them, such as when we were moving them to larger pens. I filled my mind with the images of a lynx running free in a meadow white with fresh fallen snow, averting my glance at the lynx who interpreted a direct stare as a challenge. Maybe this was pure nonsense, but it did appear that the lynx were more calm when I did this.

I believe that there was a day not long ago when humans were more in touch with their mental abilities, and were maybe not always capable of literal communication with animals, but at least capable of conveying the intense feelings of fear and respect. Anyone who has ever known horses can agree that animals are definitely capable of interpreting our most basic feelings. So I spent that night driving the dark two-lane roads leading into the wilderness, flooding my mind and heart with the images that I hoped our two wild passengers could understand. Finally, we reached our turn-off and drove the last few miles to the washed-out dirt road that led to the heart of possibly the US's last lynx stronghold.

Arriving in the early morning hours, we elected to grab a few hours of sleep before beginning the fifteen mile trek to our targeted release site. As the sun rose on a bright new day, it was like awakening not from a dream, but into one. All around us old growth cedar trees were draped with moss, and the song of the nearby river was like a lullaby enchanting us off into a wilderness fairy-land. Everyone was in their highest spirits, and after a quick review of our maps we unloaded our two lynx relations, strapped our backpacks on and began the lynx's last leg of their journey to freedom.

While four liberators carried the two boxes, I sped ahead on my mountain bike to ensure there were no other people on the trails who might raise an alarm at seeing four people carrying two lynx in boxes. Many times I had to throw my bike over my shoulder and climb over fallen trees, and as the miles passed, it became plainly evident that nature was reclaiming these isolated lands. But nothing would prove this more than the sight I was about to see. As I sped along on my bike, my senses sharpened only for the sight of another human, I glanced down on the now abandoned road I followed and saw the unmistakable tracks of a large wild cat.

Coming to a stop, I inspected the fresh tracks which brazenly led right down the center of the abandoned road. The space between each pad was the telltale sign that the tracks I was looking at belonged to a lynx. I photographed them and after finishing my reconnaissance without having seen another human, sped back to the crew carrying the lynx to lend a hand and give them the good news. As I rounded a bend in the road, I almost laughed at the suspicious looking entourage the liberators made. Three women and one man carrying two separate boxes that were covered as if they were slaves in a far-off land carrying a loyal litter containing hidden treasures. I ditched my bike along the road and switched off with one of the carriers who was tiring.

All day long we trudged along the former road, lifting the boxes over fallen trees and forging small streams. The lynx were pretty quiet about the whole affair, only occasionally swatting the sides of the box with their huge furry paws. Every couple hours we would rest in the shade and fill the lynx's water dishes which we could access through a small slit in the tarp that covered the boxes. During these breaks we would take in the beauty around us, letting our soreness and pain be forgotten as we each imagined how rightfully these lynx belonged in this wilderness. We were alone in the wilderness. It was still too early in the year for hikers or backpackers, the snow only recently melted from most roads. There was a chill in the air, and ours were the only human voices for perhaps miles. The further we got along on the road the more obstructed it became.

It was plain to see why the wild lynx whose tracks I had seen had reclaimed these ancient homelands. They were rightfully theirs, and in the absence of human intrusion, they found all they needed to survive. As the day neared its end we came across another lynx trail, this on well dotted with the trail of fur from some preyed upon animal. Finally we had covered 13 miles and decided to set up camp for the night. The lynx were moved some distance away from our camp, but still within sight. Tired and sore we fell onto the ground and into our sleeping bags to rest before the big day tomorrow. In the early morning we rose and left our camp supplies where they lay as we had only a couple of miles to go to reach the release site.

By now we had left even the abandoned road and were now on trail. Our path became more obscure and the lynx were more restless after now almost two days in their boxes. We decided to release the lynx as soon as we had reached a small clearing in the forest I had scouted the previous day. Once we reached the clearing, we placed the lynx near a small stream where they could drink if they wanted and then began to spread feces we had bright from the sanctuary so the lynx would recognize this place as their new home.

After a couple of hours of quiet we all gathered on a large boulder overlooking the clearing some distance away. We were giddy with excitement as the moment each of us had waited for for months arrived. Some us had been involved with animal liberation actions, but nothing could prepare us for the return of two prisoners to their homeland. This was an action in response to each of our own personal sorrows we held for what was quickly becoming one of the last wild nations.

Our generation was the first to see so many species in the prisons we call zoos and fur farms, or worse, not to see some species at all. A door was closing, one that in the past led to a world where animals and humans lived harmoniously. And as that door closed with each clear-cut forest or dammed river, we fell further away from ever realizing the dream our ancestors lived. The liberation and release of these few fur farm prisoners was our small attempt at holding that door open long enough for others to realize what we were losing and come to the aid of our persecuted animal brothers and sisters.

The moment arrived to open the boxes. I looked at everyone to ensure that they were ready, and climbed down from the rock and slowly approached the two lynx boxes. Standing between the boxes, I prayed silently to the earth spirits, begging for the protection of these two gentle spirits who were now returning home. We had followed all the instructions we had in our hearts and minds, and as given by the Blackfoot Medicine Woman. The night before we had smudged the two lynx and now it was time to turn over any control to the earth mother.

Grabbing each box door in one hand, I slid them open at the same time and quickly retreated back to the boulder. As soon as the boxes opened, the lynx were out. Not running, but out. They stared first at each other, appearing like a mirror image and then began scanning their surroundings from the stream that trickled before them to the cedar tree canopy a hundred feet in the sky. They never looked back. Slowly they began to investigate their new home, stepping gingerly over logs, sipping the fresh water in the stream and within ten minutes melted into the forest around them, one following the other. They were gone. Maybe they would starve, or be killed by another lynx or some other predator. But then again, maybe, just maybe they would dig into their genetic memory and hunt the snowshoe hare, forget months in captivity and have kittens and live. Really live. No human would ever decide the fate of these two animals. Liberation for them meant the total independence from human interference.

Wildlife rehabilitators had told us of the ability of domestic cats to survive in the wild, and in their opinion bobcats and lynx had even more going for them. What they needed most was isolation from humans. Introducing wild animals into their diet had taught them to see other animals as food, not something handed to them dead already. Placing the lynx in large enclosures had allowed them to develop muscular strength that was not possible in the small cages on the fur farm, and isolating them from human view had reinforced their fear of humans.

I like to think that for the lynx released, one of their greatest freedoms was to never run to the end of their cages. When we obtained them their cages got larger and larger and finally their last residence would be the largest roadless area left in their range in the lower 48 states. I hope they ran and jumped, drank sweet spring waters and munched the tasty flesh of yearling snowshoe hares who lived in abundance in the spring of 1991. I like to think that the lynx had kittens who would never see a human being. Kittens who would only know the world of their great-grandparents. And when the day came when our former lynx friends crossed over into the lynx spirit world, I hope all their memories were of being a lynx, not any within a cage.

Later that night we all returned to our campsite, broke down the now empty lynx boxes and sat around the campfire lost in our own thoughts. Without the lynx I felt like a visitor in a world I would probably never quite fully understand. Around the campfire we talked about food (as ours had run out) and sang songs from our urban eco-warrior culture, mostly punk rock songs about smashing the state and animal liberation. We were the lost children of the earth, but we were struggling to find our own way home as the lynx now had.

That night we all fell asleep early, rolled in our sleeping bags which were sprawled around the now dead campfire. As I tried to sleep I could not help but recognize the fear I had not felt since I was a child camping in the wilderness. I felt that something was out there, just outside of sight. I laughed to myself and rolled over and tried to sleep, but the fear would not go away. Then I heard it. It was a low-throated growl that I tried hard to believe was the river. Then it was closer. First in front of me, then behind me. In the moonless night all I could hear was, "GRrrrrr...." as it moved around the campsite. Finally the sound disappeared and one by one we began to whisper, "did you hear that!?" not even knowing whether anyone was awake. We all were and had all heard it.

Then it dawned on us. Amongst our camp gear were empty boxes with their lynx scent and the bags we had used to carry lynx feces; it was a scent siren to every wild lynx in the area. We had been visited by a native lynx who recognized the smell of one of her own.

We were indeed only visitors to this enchanted world where the Lynx Nation reigned supreme and it felt good to feel fear towards an animal who had visited us on its own terms not ours. We returned to our own world, to the cities and freeways, the world where the only lynx were hanging from coat racks in posh department stores and fur boutiques.

And back in Ronan, Montana the lynx still pace their cages, staring at the wilderness they once called home. They remain prisoners of a war that began when the first European set foot in their world spreading jaws of steel that would begin to bite away at their peaceful nation. And it is a war that continues today on any one of hundreds of fur farms and traplines near you. What remains to be seen is whether the children of the earth will break from the ranks of the culture of death and join us in trying to hold open the door to the world that is quickly disappearing, leaving us alone in a world where only Man and his machines reign supreme.

DEAD BUFFALO

*W*hen European fur traders invaded the North American continent it wasn't long before they had begun to push many of the animal people close to extinction. By the 1800s the beaver nation was so depleted that the fur trade began to shift its focus to the immense bison herds that blanketed the Great Plains. By the 1830s bison hides became the most sought-after animal fur in the American West. The next sixty years would see one of mankind's most atrocious onslaughts against wildlife as bison herds that once numbered sixty million or more were reduced to less than 1,000 in the entire nation. Commercial hunters would slaughter thousands each day, stripping only their hides and tongues and leaving the rest to rot.

Bison were not the only beings targeted for extermination at this time on the Great Plains. By the 1870s the US military was engaged in a campaign of genocide against the indigenous peoples of the Lakota, Cheyenne, Arapaho and other nations all of whom depended on the bison for spiritual and physical sustenance.

General Phil Sheridan developed the policy whereby millions of bison would be slaughtered to deny indigenous nations the food, shelter and clothing they needed to survive. He was to say of the commercial slaughter, "These men [buffalo hunters] have done in the last two years, and will do in the next year, and more to settle the vexed Indian question than the entire regular army has done in the last thirty years."

With a deadly prophetic vision he would also say, "They are destroying the Indians commissary; and it is a well-known fact that an army losing its base of supplies is placed at a great disadvantage... let them kill, skin and sell until the buffaloes are exterminated. Then your prairies can be covered with speckled cattle..."

The great warriors of the Lakota nation; Sitting Bull and Crazy Horse would go to war in what they sometimes called "The war to save the buffalo" and fought valiantly against the hide hunters and US soldiers intent on destroying the central being of their culture, spirituality and very existence.

In the Lakota culture it was a white buffalo that transformed into a woman who delivered to their people the seven sacred ceremonial rites that Sheridan and the US were intent on destroying. Their noble resistance was defeated and as the bison disappeared so did the ability of many indigenous people to survive.

By the 1890s the vast herds that stretched from horizon to horizon and made the land seem to be alive with their movement had all but been wiped out. Their destruction was a calculated chapter of Manifest Destiny that sought to eradicate both the bison and the cultures and way of life that the indigenous peoples who worshipped them believed in.

As the bison herds vanished they were replaced by domestic cattle who quickly rose in dominance among the Euroamerican culture and economy where they remain today.

A mountain of buffalo skulls

At the close of the 19th Century, a small herd of less than 30 bison was discovered to be hidden in the high valleys and forests of the Yellowstone area. Yellowstone National Park, before it was stolen in violation of congressional treaties with indigenous nations was the home of many tribes.

After their forced relocation to reservations in the Oklahoma Territory a band of Cheyenne attempted an exodus back to Yellowstone area leaving behind the starvation and disease of the reservation. In the midst of winter hundreds of Cheyenne, mostly women and children broke away and crossed the plains where they were hunted down and slaughtered by US troops before finally surrendering and returning to the reservation.

Though the people who lived in harmony with the Buffalo Nation had also been nearly exterminated like their four-legged relations, many survived on scattered reservation across the Great Plains. They were both to share the struggle for survival in that dark chapter in US history that was the early 20th century.

Meanwhile, the bison tribe that had found sanctuary in Yellowstone began to grow. In 1917 the small bison herd had become infected with brucellosis by the "speckled cattle" that had replaced them on their former range. In the 1940s a ban was placed on the live transportation of Yellowstone bison to area indigenous tribes at the bequest of the cattle industry who feared a brucellosis outbreak. Previous to the ban Yellowstone bison had provided the tribes with the handful of animals that would eventually become many of the herds that exist today.

The bison of Yellowstone were managed much like cattle through the 1950s and 60s, they were herded and penned, fed hay in the winter and when their numbers grew they were slaughtered. By the late 1960s with their numbers at just 400, Yellow Stone park officials allowed bison and nature a longer leash and the bison were allowed to resume a more natural migration, leaving the park in the winter in search of grazing lands at lower elevations, but returning to the park in the springtime.

In 1985 the USDA's Animal and Plant Health Inspection Service (APHIS) declared Montana's cattle "brucellosis-free" and began to pressure the state of Montana and Yellowstone National Park to kill or control any bison that left the park boundaries. So was to begin the second war to exterminate free-roaming bison.

At the heart of the present day controversy is the unsubstantiated hysteria created by the APHIS that if allowed to road freely outside of Yellowstone, the bison will transmit brucellosis.

APHIS is also the parent agency to the notorious Animal Damage Control USDA program that annually kills tens of thousands of native predators who the livestock industry claim also threaten their profits. APHIS is also funding animal research into disease that impedes the growth of the livestock industry. These experiments are conducted on bison, elk, deer, bighorn sheep, coyotes and other animals at federal research facilities across the west and at universities such as Washington State in Pullman and Utah State in Logan.

Since 1985 APHIS has led the battle against the Yellowstone bison herd threatening to remove Montana's brucellosis-free status that has cost cattlemen millions and allows them to avoid costly inspections when exporting cattle out of state and the country.

Despite many bison and elk in Montana carrying the brucellosis bacteria, there has yet to be even one documented case of transmission from bison to cattle anywhere outside of laboratories.

Brucellosis, which can only be transmitted to cattle from the fresh afterbirth of bison, can cause pregnant cows to abort their fetuses costing the cattle industry potential profits from lost beef production. Brucellosis can be carried by many species of wildlife who scavenge the afterbirth of bison who can become infected but not infectious. In 1989, 900 bison left Yellowstone and scattered among cattle. Montana later tested the cattle and 20 other herds for brucellosis and found no evidence of the bacteria.

In 1988 over 500 bison were shot by private hunters and game wardens. Following the slaughter of the later 1980s, Yellowstone Park officials, the state of Montana and

APHIS began the eradication program that exists today, all with the justification of preventing a brucellosis outbreak.

In the winter of 1991-92, of 218 bison slaughtered none were infectious animals capable of transmission.

By the minter of 1993 the combined governmental and private forces that had enacted a "shoot-on-sight" policy towards bison leaving Yellowstone. These included not just infectious females (the only bison capable of Brucellosis transmission) but also young and old males and calves.

It must be remembered that in many cases the bison who leave Yellowstone do not immediately enter onto private lands. Much of the killing is done on national forest lands that are leased to cattlemen at below market value. It is no secret that cattle receive more protection on public lands than native wildlife.

Coupled with these obvious deceptions is also the fact that when bison who are infectious are giving birth in the springtime, they are inside the park boundaries and far from grazing cattle.

Bison are naturally gregarious animals, roaming freely from range to range and knocking down any fences that stand in their path. They are not the docile beasts cattlemen have bred cows to be. Park boundaries and the special interest politics of the USDA and the state of Montana with its powerful livestock industry refuse to allow for the natural habits and migrations of wildlife such as Yellowstone bison herd.

The slaughter of Yellowstone bison begins to look like nothing other than a renewed effort by the US government and the livestock industry to control or eradicate any potential free-roaming herds of native grazing animals that they believe not only threaten their economic grasp on western lands, but also represent a resurgence of indigenous wildlife and the people whose beliefs allow them to live harmoniously.

This slaughter continues today, and the government does not look likely to end it of its own free will.

CANADIAN

SEAL WARS

*E*very spring, the Harp Seal Nation begins an annual migration that takes its Western population from the High Arctic south, into the waters of what is now Canada, to the Gulf of Saint Lawrence and off the Newfoundland Coast. These seals rarely if ever come ashore, choosing instead to give birth on the massive ice floes that drift off the northeastern coast of the Atlantic seaboard.

They once numbered in the tens of millions living in balanced harmony with the Whale and Finned Fish Nations in an abundance almost beyond the imagination. A French trader in 1760 reported seeing harp seals off the northern tip of Newfoundland, filling the sea from shore to horizon in their spring migration south for ten solid days and nights.

Once arrived on the ice flow nurseries, harp seal mothers give birth to a single pup which will molt in two weeks, living off the fat reserves built up with the mother's rich milk. At five to six weeks the pup enters the water, learning how to swim and feed her/himself. At the end of the birthing and breading season, adult harp seals gather on the ice flows collectively to socialize and sun themselves before beginning the long journey back to their Arctic home.

Since time immemorial, Inuit hunters had subsisted on the immense harp seal population, taking only what they needed for survival in their unforgiving environment. This was, unfortunately, not to be the limits of human-to-seal relations.

As early as 1700, French colonists developed a harp seal fishery and began a war of commercial exploitation that led to a campaign of extermination against the Inuit themselves, in order to gain complete control of northern Newfoundland and her rich diversity of wildlife.

But the French were only pioneers, as they have been in most of the fur trade in the New World, and by the 1730s, the English had moved in and begun their own harp seal fishery, marketing, like the French, predominantly the seal's oil rendered from the thick layers of fat on young harp seals. By the 1770s, sealers had ventured onto the ice floe nurseries and began the slaughter of harp seal pup that continues to this day.

By the turn of the 19th Century, the combined French and English kill using nets and clubs exceeded 100,000 animals, rising to 280,000 by 1819.

In 1840, one eyewitness described the slaughter: "One of the men hooked up a young seal with his gaff. Its cries were precisely like those of a young child in the

extremity of agony and distress, something between shrieks and convulsive sobbing... I saw one poor wretch skinned while yet alive, and the body writhing in blood after being stripped of its pelt... the vision of another writhing its snow-white wooly body with its head bathed in blood, through which it was vainly endeavoring to see and breathe, really haunting my dreams."

By then, shooting had become the most common way to kill seals (as it remains today) with adults providing the majority of oil. The most experienced sealer recovered only about one out of every five seals shot, meaning that then and now the total number of harp seals killed is as much as triple of what is reported.

In the spring of 1844, approximately 740,000 harp seals were killed just from the Newfoundland, Labrador and Gulf of St. Lawrence slaughters; further north along the Greenland coast Germans, Danes, Dutch and Norwegians joined in the killing, slaughtering tens of thousands more seals.

The pure greed of an example sealing industry spared no seal, young or old. Infants a few days old and even pregnant mothers were killed before the next sealer could reach them. "Never leave nothing to the devil" was the motto of the 19th Century sealer.

Often this greed would result in tens of thousands of seals killed and wasted, when their pelts piled by sealers could not be reached by the sealers' ships. By the middle of the 1800s, as many as 1,000,000 harp seals were being slaughtered annually.

Early in the 1850s, in an era referred to in Newfoundland history as the "Great Days of Sealing" the European demand for harp seals last remaining ice floe nursery.

By the 1890s, the harp seal nation began to collapse, with repeated years of over a million seals killed annually causing sealers to kill "only" about 250,00 until World War One. The war effort that turned its carnage against other humans instead of seals cost the sealing industry most of its fleets of ships and though sealing continued on a largely reduced scale, it was to remain a show of what it once was until World War Two, when there was an almost complete cessation in the War against the Harp Seal Nation. The peace was temporary.

In 1946, the Norwegian Karl Karlsen established the Karlsen Shipping Company in Nova Scotia. Already proven as a butcher of the Great Whale Nations and of the Harp and Hood Seal tribes further north in the Arctic, Karlsen helped lead the modern war on the seals that continues today.

By 1950, the Newfoundlanders rejoined the slaughter begun again by Karlsen with an additional 14 Norwegian killer ships, which drove the harp seal kill up to over 200,000. A year later it would double.

By 1961, the western harp seal population was estimated to be 1,750,000, half of what it had been only ten years earlier and but a mere fraction of what it was before European exploitation. In the mid-1960s, sealers began to use helicopters and light aircraft to ferry sealers to the nurseries, while the Canadian Government offered aerial reconnaissance and Coast Guard ice breakers to cut a swathe through thick ice for smaller sealing vessels.

In the rapacious bloodbath fueled by the international fur trade, conservation and humane slaughter were (and today are) completely absent. Greed ruled the ice and unspeakable cruelty was the rule as thousands of seal pups were skinned alive or wasted because of get-rich-quick inexperienced skinners.

In 1964, an estimated 85% of all seal pups born were slaughtered off the Labrador Coast and 81,000 were killed in the Gulf of St. Lawrence. Some sealers reported a kill ratio of one in ten for every seal shot. The total kill rose to 500,000 harp and hood seals.

In 1966, the first non-governmental observers were allowed to witness the slaughter of a small fraction of the 385,000 seals killed and concluded that as many as half of all harp seal pups killed were being skinned alive.

In 1967, the only efforts made to regulate the slaughter were ignored when quotas for pups were exceeded by 100% to 100,000 in the Gulf alone, while another 232,000 harp and hooded seals (mostly pups) were killed off the Labrador Coast.

In 1968, author Farley Mowat, after witnessing the kill called it an "orgy of destruction conducted by, and for, people who were prepared to commit or to countenance almost any degree of savagery in order to maintain a high rate of profitability."

In 1969 and 1970, the kill totaled 300,000 harp and hooded seals. In response to mounting public opposition to the seal slaughter, the Canadian Government established the "Seal Protection Act" which ironically did nothing to protect seals but everything to protect sealers.

Under the new regulations no unauthorized aircraft could fly below 2,000 ft over the seal nurseries or land within 2 nautical miles of any seal, literally meaning anywhere near the slaughter. These regulations in effect prohibited anyone but seal killers access to ice floes where others such as the media and non-governmental observers had exposed the slaughter to the international public.

By the time the Canadian, Danish and Norwegian Governments established quotas in 1971, the sealers were unable to fill them due to the ever increasing collapse of harp and hooded seal populations.

When the quotas were reduced even further in 1972, again the sealers were unable to reach it. And again in 1973. In the mid-1970s the western harp seal population was estimated at less than a million and in 1976 the quota was reduced to 127,000.

A journalist illegally flown into the seal slaughter wrote:

There's this mother seal ten feet away from me, she's rocking back and forth, lifting her mouth to the sky and keening. By her belly is a plum-colored heap of meat, all that remains of her infant. As I watch her the crying ceases.

She makes no further sound, though she seems to be trying. It's like a battlefield. As far as you can see the ice is splashed with blood. On the horizon, in black silhouette, men are swinging clubs up and down in the white glare.

The tiny carcasses of whitecoats, not much bigger than a good-sized roast once the fur and fat are taken, stare at us with the bulging eyes protruding from heads smashed by sealers' clubs.

We walk toward a flag and happen on a truly horrible scene; a mother seal whose head has been smashed, whose snout has been driven sideways, and who is still alive, breathing shallowly through her battered face.

What we're watching is comparable to killing kittens with claw hammers; it can't be called a hunt.

When the group of journalists returned to land, they were arrested and charged with violating the Seal Protection Act.

In 1976, a group of Greenpeace activists led by 26 year old Canadian Paul Watson illegally flew into the hunt and placed their bodies between the seals and the sealers before the helicopters used to transport them were forcibly grounded. Watson and comrade Robert Hunter then stood in the path of a sealing ship crashing through the ice, forcing it to stop before he too could be arrested and charged with violating the Seal Protection Act. The following year an amendment was passed making it illegal to also interfere with the killing of any seal.

In 1977, the quota was increased to 170,000 despite the fact that experts predicted the western harp seal would be pushed into extinction if the slaughter continued. That same year Paul Watson and fellow Greenpeace members returned to the slaughter. After taking a club from a sealers hand and throwing it in the water, Watson chained himself to a winch line used to haul seal pelts aboard a sealing ship. He was dragged through the icy waters by sealers yelling "Kill him! Kill him!"

His action on the ice that year were considered "too violent" by the Greenpeace Board of Directors. Watson, a founding member of the organization, was asked to leave.

The spring of 1979 saw something never before seen in the harp seal nurseries. A new ship was on the horizon, this one with the mission of saving seals instead of killing them. On her bow was the name Sea Shepherd and the captain was none other than Watson.

Before the Sea Shepherd could be stopped, over 1,000 harp seal pups had been sprayed with a harmless dye that rendered their fur worthless, at least to the sealers. The crew was eventually arrested and once again found to be violating the dubious Seal Protection Act.

The Sea Shepherd would later be sunk in Portugal after Watson had rammed the world's most notorious pirate whaling ship, which was later blown up in harbor without injuries.

By 1980, the Canadian Government had swung its propaganda machine into full gear, over-inflating harp seal estimates and warning that unless more seals were killed, the Atlantic fisheries would be threatened by the fish-eating seals. No finger of blame for the depleted fish numbers was pointed towards the factory trawlers of the commercial fishing industry who for decades had been raping the North Atlantic seas of all her aquatic life.

In 1981, 250,000 harp and hooded seals were slaughtered in Canada. To preserve its barbaric trade in seal fur, the Canadian Government was forced to lobby against a proposed European Economic Community ban on seal pup pelts, and threatened to continue the hunt alone should the commercial market be destroyed.

Farley Mowat writes of the denial, "This new massacre of seals is based, as all previous ones have been, on a campaign of falsification, vilification and outright lies worthy of Joseph Goebbel [Nazi propagandist]."

In 1985, I joined the crew of the Sea Shepherd in Halifax, Nova Scotia, the home port of the Karlsen Shipping Co. and where the Sea Shepherd had sat for two years following its confiscation in 1983.

As we sailed off the coast of Newfoundland I read tales of multitudes of whales and seals so great that they posed a hazard to navigation by the newly arriving Europeans. I would then scan the very same horizon and maybe see one distant gull and if fortunate a rare whale or dolphin. Needless to say I was greatly saddened at the emptiness brought own by man's continuing war against nature.

The Canadian seal slaughter is more than the world's largest slaughter of marine mammals; it represents man's about-face march he has taken in his interaction with non-human animals. Since the days of harmony, greed has blackened the hearts of men making them either apathetic or numb to the harm their actions have on the natural world.

The representation of callousness brought upon man by slaughtering so many unmistakably innocent creatures in their stage of vulnerability, infancy, cannot be ignored from being symptomatic of a much greater problem threatening our world today.

Apologists for the earth destroyers and animal abusers are quick to point to naturally-caused cases of extinction, but no one can deny that never before in the history of earth has there been such an accelerated rate of extinction as that caused by modern man.

The Canadian Seal Wars are just one regionalized armed conflict that happens to be particularly brutal in visibility to any who questions its impact on the other beings we share our planet with.

Indigenous peoples with generations invested into observation of the natural world and our place within it could have told us what scientists and biologists are now confirming. That is simply that our impact on one species—be it the cod decimated by industrialized over-fishing or harp and hooded seal slaughtered for fur, oil or as scapegoats—will surely lead to imbalance, threatening the entire delicate ecological integrity of the world's oceans with collapse.

Already, federal subsidies helped build new sealing boats and the Canadian Coast Guard and Fisheries Service were assisting sealers with ice and weather forecasts, aerial reconnaissance to locate the seal nurseries and millions spent to monitor, regulate and promote the slaughter.

While accusations were made that harp seals threatened the fisheries, the Canadian Government ignored the fact that harp seals feed on non-commercial fish who actually prey on commercial fish, and nursing seals fast while in Canadian waters. This balance between seals and fish explains why previous to commercial exploitation, tens of millions of seals coexisted with what were some of the world's most abundant fish populations. Early colonists recorded that cod fish were in such abundance that all one had to do to catch them was toss a bucket with a line into the water and pull out the fish.

In 1982, despite Canada's threat to restrict EEC member nations' fishing rights in its waters, an EEC ban on the importation of harp and hooded seal pup pelts was passed, but the band would only last two years. Later, loopholes would be created to render the ban completely useless.

The 1983 quota was set at 180,000 harp and 12,000 hooded seals. Newfoundland's Minister of Fisheries instructed sealers to kill 100,000 seals or the cod fishery would be destroyed, and stated that his department would pay half a million to help subsidize the purchase of pelts bought by the Karlsen Shipping Co. and the pelt-buyer Carino Ltd.

The Sea Shepherd's 1983 campaign came at the time when other protest pressure was threatening a boycott of Canadian fish in the UK. The combination of opposition from all angles, plus the EEC ban on seal pup pelts resulted in less than half of the 1983 seal quota being filled.

In 1984, continuing pressure from all sides resulted in only 3,000 seals being killed out of a quota of 200,000. By 1987, the killing of harp and hooded seal newborns finally stopped, but 60,000 seals a year–many as young as four to six weeks old, yet labeled as adults–continued to be killed.

Unfortunately for the Harp Seal Nation, no sooner did the European market for seal pup fur collapse than a new market in the late 1980s was being explored in the Far East. In 1994, Terra Nova Fisheries Co. of St. Johns, Newfoundland sold 50,000 seals to a Shanghai company allegedly for their pelts and meat, but in reality for the penises which are dried and sold in Asian herb shops worldwide for as much as $200. Joining the largely illegal trade in other wildlife parts, seal penises are marketed as aphrodisiacs.

In 1995, Paul Watson returned to the seal hunt without a ship, but was beaten in the Magdalen Islands by an angry mob of sealers while the Canadian police and Fisheries officers stood by and did nothing. That year 66,000 harp and hooded seals were killed from a 186,000 quota.

Sea Shepherd has repeatedly tried to promote an ecologically-friendly practice whereby baby seals are painlessly brushed of their molting fur, which is then sold as insulation material in European-made garments. But Canadian sealers such as those in the Magdalen Islands have expressed their intent to kill seals rather than brush them.

There is also a growing tourism industry that produces sizable incomes to sealers who would guide foreign tourists onto the ice floes to see live harp seal pups, but this

economic alternative also is resisted by the
Canadian Government, which appears
intent on wiping out Canada's eastern
Atlantic seal populations.

In 1996, encouraged by the new
Asian market, the Department of Fisheries
and Oceans increased the seal quota to
250,000 and allowed for the first time in
20 years the use of aircraft in the slaughter
and the return of Norwegian killer ships.
This resulted in the first large scale
slaughter since the EEC ban of 1983 and
cost 243,000 harp and 27,000 hooded
seals their lives.

Animal welfare investigators filmed
over 144 violations of Canada's Marine
Mammal Regulations such as gaffs used
to hook live seals, seals flopping on the
ice spouting blood from bullet wounds,
skinning alive seals and killing them only
for their genitalia.

The market for seals in 1996 began
to expand again with pelts fetching $20,
the meat being used for novelty sausage and pepperoni, with a large quantity being
sold to Canadian fur farms. Irregardless of the band on killing seal pups, Mark Small,
the president of the Canadian Sealers Association was revealed to be the supplier in
an operation that killed 25,000 newborn seal pups as part of an illegal Newfoundland
trade which dealt with Norwegian fur-buyers.

In 1997, CSA officials claimed that Norway's Carino Co. alone requested 200,000
seal pelts of the 250,000 quota from the previous year. As well as raising quotas and
subsidizing the sale of seal meat, the Canadian Government also replaced the SPA,
which was ruled unconstitutional following Sea Shepherd's court battle; replacing
it was identical "fishing" regulations continuing to make it a crime punishable with
up to two years in prison to witness the killing of a seal. Also, at a November, 1997
fisheries exposition, a Norwegian company sold its entire stock of seal penises to a
Singapore businessman who has guaranteed a market for seal penises from the 1998
slaughter.

Newfoundland Fisheries Minster, John Efford, also had been promoting seal
products in China, Thailand, Japan and Korea and recently told journalists, "If we
do our marketing right and get into those countries, in five, ten years down the road
sealing could be worth at least $100 million a year. The Chinese people are looking
for new products; new meat and new species of animals such as seals and other marine
mammals. And we have it here, so we have to get it into their country."

In Canada itself, seal product distributor JW Hiscock and Sons and Briggets
says it will target Asian communities in Toronto and Vancouver. The 1998 Canadian

harp and hooded seal slaughter quota has been set at 275,000 the same as 1997 which it is believed was exceeded by over 80% taking into account seals killed but not recovered.

Caboto Seafoods Ltd. is responding to the revitalized seal wars by remodeling a fish processing plant in Newfoundland into a sealing plant to extract oil from carcasses and tan pelts for sale to buyers like Norway's Carino Ltd. The seal slaughter this year will receive $500,000 in direct federal subsidies with indirect subside meat grants to the Canadian Sealers Association and seal processors such as Caboto, and other elements of the sealing industry, bringing all federal funding well over $3.5 million or between $28,000-34,000 for less than 200 full-time jobs created by killing seals.

The Canadian Government argues that the seal slaughter is a necessary measure to conserve fish populations that have failed to rebound despite a commercial moratorium enacted in the early 1990s. Meanwhile, a petition by 97 biologists from 15 countries, who comprise the Society for Marine Mamalogist, condemned Canada's seal kill stating, "All scientific efforts have failed to show any impact. Over fishing remains the only scientifically demonstrated problem."

The Canadian commercial fishing industry appears to be in serious denial of their own impact on the marine environment, continually believing that if they kill enough seals the fish populations will return and their economic greed can be satiated.

The wholesale rape of the marine eco-system off Canada's coast may be irreparable as is suggested by a marine biologist who has studied the impact of commercial drag netters who tear up the ocean floor, displacing hydroids, a tiny cousin of jellyfish. The hydroids have been found in dense concentrations at middle-depths normally occupied by commercially valuable cod and haddock, where they eat not only capepods, the main food source of cod and haddock, but also the commercial fishes own larvae, contributing additionally to the fishes decline due directly to over fishing

Destroying the Finned Nations does not seem to be enough for the Canadian fishing industry; they must also destroy the Seal Nations as a scapegoat rather than accept responsibility for their own actions over the last couple of hundred years.

As man exhausts one species of fish commercially and then turns to the next link in the ocean's food chain for exploitation, as the commercial fishing industry is doing in the North Atlantic, he slowly removes the integral blocks which make up the very foundation that sustains all life in the seas.

With the consumers of commercially harvested fish out of sight and out of mind to the impact their diet is having on the ocean ecosystem, we are edging ever closer to a dangerous ecological threshold with an effect beyond our imagination. For those who choose life for the oceans and all future generations, only one thing can return us to a level of coexistence and harmony that will bring about an end to the wars against the nations that live in the sea.

For the seal people, I think back to the stories I have heard from places like Scotland and Ireland, where oral traditions preserve memories of the times not long ago when the seal king and queen and the silkies, seal people, lived in the world of humans. I recall the story of a horseman who called on a sealer's daughter to come to the aid of her father in danger upon the sea.

The horseman led her to a cliff overlooking her father's boat on the storm-tossed sea and together they plunged into the waters where the horseman was transformed into a seal. She was led along roads of coral to a great pearl castle where many other seal people were crying over a beautiful young seal woman with a knife stuck deep inside her.

The girl was called upon to remove it as her father was responsible for trying to kill the seal woman who now lay in agony. She felt the seals pain as she removed the knife and was brought to the surface of the sea where her troubled father witnessed her own transformation from seal to girl as she came to his rescue. He swore to God never again to harm another seal.

There are many more stories of seals saving drowning sailors, sheltering and suckling human infants, wedding lonely fisherman and other tales of love and compassion between the seal and human nations. These are not simple myths or children's stories, they are fleeting reminders of a life we once shared with the seal nations, which are more important to our survival than any monetary wealth or employment accumulated by commercial fishing or seal slaughter.

Such memories are the cries of the seal people calling on us to return to the life where we realize that the war against the seals, the war against nature, is also a war that destroys our own spirit, ruining forever the finned, flippered and five-fingered peoples' hope for peace.

THE EZLN AND
INDIAN AUTONOMY

*M*y job here in prison is with landscaping. I rake, sweep and water plants, and generally keep my designated area clean. It's very meditative and I work alone which means I think a lot to myself. There's a cactus wren nest I watch out for, and tarantulas, scorpions, mice, hummingbirds and grackles that call this place home and I try to make sure they get enough food and water. From where I work I can see the Black Mountains where my village lies, and through the mountains, trees, plants and animals I can never forget why I am here:

I was at a Pow-Wow on New Years Day, 1994 when I heard that Indians in southern Mexico had seized six towns in the state of Chiapas in an early morning declaration of war against the Mexican government. Excitedly, I exchanged expressions with other indigenous brothers and sisters acknowledging this Indian uprising as the first of my generations. Our hearts swelled as Yaqui friends and I watched videos of ski-mask clad rebels with their trademark red bandanas marching in formation, many of them clearly women. The struggle in Chiapas is the result of hundreds of years of oppression that has left the proud Mayan Nation without land, liberty or justice. Not to mention no education, health care, housing, clean water, jobs or basic human rights. As indigenous peoples in the "First World" the Zapatista Army for National Liberation (EZLN) and their armed struggle means much, especially to me and my Yaqui relations. After all, it was not long ago that our own great-grandparents were fighting a guerilla war against the same government for the very same things.

I was tempted to run to Chiapas and join this new rebellion. It would have been easy. I was wanted in the US by the government and prison was on my horizon. A new life in the southern jungles of Mexico didn't sound too bad. A noble life, and a dignified death, what more can a young indigenous revolutionary ask for? An aid

caravan from the Pomo Nation in California was in Tucson and some of us Yaquis hosted them in our tribe's senior center where my elders gave them our blessings. The next day as I helped the Pomos pack the last truck, I said goodbye to the thought of running away to Chiapas. Because running away is what I'd be doing. We need to rally our own people and communities in the same way that the Zapatistas have. We need to begin building the framework to support our own resistance while at the same time lending aid to our southern relations.

The EZLN spent ten years preparing for their uprising; organizing, teaching, building and planning. It is all too common for us Americans(sic) to ride the wave of other peoples' resistance rather than building our own. Like the EZLN all peoples–not just Indians–should reclaim their lives and build their own health clinics, schools, adult literacy programs, women's rights, day-care centers, self defense training projects and return to a true grassroots democracy such as existed before European conquest. The Zapatistas have in this way shown us in the Global North all that we must do to secure a future for our people. "Everything for everyone, nothing for ourselves…" read the communiqués from the jungles of Chiapas, and as Zapatistas have so proudly proven, it is better to die on your feet than live on your knees.

And it wasn't long before the US government sent in the cavalry once again. This time it has to be a little less obvious so it began with military hardware to be used to snuff out our relations in the South. A $40 billion bail out of Mexican economy by the US alone did not come without strings attached. Now US military advisors have been reported in Chiapas, just like Vietnam. And the troubles are not limited to Chiapas. Now a new guerrilla army has emerged in Mexico, less diplomatic than the EZLN, the Popular Revolutionary Army (ERP) has attacked police stations and military installations killing 41 Mexican soldiers and wounding 43 others. The failure of the Mexican state to control its peasant population will almost inevitably lead to greater US military support and participation in the new Indian Wars.

The National Commission for Democracy in Mexico released a report on US government and military involvement in Mexico's "low intensity war" in 1995. It detailed how the US is escalating its donation of arms and war materials to the Mexican military, of which one quarter (40-50,000 troops) are deployed in Chiapas. In plain English, the US is once again killing Indians. Not that they ever really stopped. Disguised as the "War on Drugs" US manufactured guns, bombs, planes and helicopters are being given to the Mexican military. The US specifically mentioned the indigenous uprising in Chiapas during its $40 billion bailout, citing the unrest as a potential barricade to free trade. Who besides multinational corporations benefit from NAFTA and military repression of Indians in Mexico? Bomb factories like

McDonnell Douglas and Hughes Missiles freely profit from the killing of Indians by manufacturing and supplying the weapons to kill them. Just as the notorious "Tucson Ring" of arms dealers profited here in Arizona by discouraging an end to the Apache Wars in the 1880s. Then and now, the US government has always initiated military action whenever indigenous peoples demand sovereignty and basic human rights.

In 1973 the US military was deployed to Wounded Knee, South Dakota when the American Indian Movement's warriors occupied the site of a massacre in 1891.

In Spring of 1995 while I was out on bail, I drove down to the Tohono O'odham reservation just south of my village in Tucson. Near the village of San Miguel only a couple miles from the Mexican border, I was shocked to see US military troops deployed in the area. When I enquired about them I was told they were given permission from the tribe to set up camp to aid in the "War on Drugs." Many of my friends who have traveled in northern Mexico near the US border have told me of the military checkpoints, road blocks and searches that are conducted, as the US and Mexican states fear that American Indians and their sympathizers will supply their own arms to the indigenous of Mexico. And so, armed with machetes and with less than 4,000 well-armed warriors the Zapatistas are fighting for freedom, democracy and justice against 40-50,000 Mexican troops armed and equipped by the US government.

Chiapas and the Zapatista rebellion is just as close to Arizona as is South Dakota, yet few people express outrage at this US-backed war on indigenous peoples in Mexico. What separates American Indians like us Yaquis from the Lakota in South Dakota is the same thing that separates us from the Mayans of Chiapas. Nothing. Just imaginary lines drawn by the politicians who have stolen our lands and destroyed our people. Our skin is brown and our blood is red. How can we as American Indians be disgraced and angered with military forces and not be outrages by the very same type of military action against indigenous peoples today? It is time for all of us to speak out against these modern Indian Wars where our people are forced to live in such poverty that inevitable military defeat is better than living a life of disrespect, denial of basic human rights and freedoms where we are forced to continually lick our invaders boots. The EZLN are our brothers and sisters and we should do everything we can to resist to US military involvement in the war against them.

Estacion Libre is an anarchist people of color EZLN solidarity group based in NYC

CUSTER'S LAST STAND

*T*o indigenous peoples, Custer was a ruthless murderer. He was known among the Lakota and Cheyenne as a butcher of women and children, ordering attacks on peaceful villages in his quest for military and political honor; and killing Indians has always, even today, been a good way to get it. It was Custer who, in blatant violation of the Fort Laramie Treaty of 1868, led an expedition into the most sacred of holy lands, the place of origin for the Lakota people, Paha Sapa, the Black Hills of what is now called South Dakota. There he discovered gold and announced it to the media, instituting a gold rush which continues to this day. When the Lakota expressed outrage at this violation of their treaty with the US government, they were offered pennies per acre for the heart of their earth mother. That money still sits in a bank and the Lakota still today refuse to accept

Illustration of Custer's massacre of a Cheyenne village

the money for their land– they want the return of what was stolen from them.

Then the Lakota attempted to evict the gold miners in the 1870s; the US military was sent in to "destroy the hostile Indians." "Hostiles" are any Indians who refused to live life in near starvation on the reservations where disease and social disorder was rampant.

In 1876, US forces engaged the hostiles on the Rosebud River and were totally routed. General Crook with whom Custer led the attack, later recounted the battle, crediting the Lakota and Cheyenne with incredible acts of bravery, including that of a woman who charged into the midst of the battlefield to rescue her wounded brother.

Two weeks later, Custer discovered an immense encampment on the Little Bighorn. Not wanting to await reinforcements from Crook, Custer ordered a charge on the camp of over 3,000. Lakota and Cheyenne warriors rallied to defend their people from the man they called "the Chief of Thieves." With shouts of, "Brave hearts forward! Coward hearts to the rear!" indigenous leaders Sitting Bull and Crazy Horse led their people to victory, completely destroying Custer's 7th Cavalry of over 200 men. Many soldiers were mutilated by the Indian women and children in retaliation for the mutilation of civilians by these very men. Custer's body was left alone because no Lakota or Cheyenne wanted to dirty themselves by touching it. Yet some Indian women took leather awls and poked holes in Custer's ears supposedly saying, "In your next life, with these added holes maybe you will listen when we tell you Lakota land is not for sale..."

The victory at Greasy Grass signaled the end of the Sioux Wars, as the whites called them. Increased military repression led to the defeat of the Lakota Nation, and one by one leaders like Crazy Horse and Sitting Bull led their battered and broken yet proud people onto reservations, where many remain today. Within a few short years hundreds more would be slaughtered after both Crazy Horse and Sitting Bull were assassinated on the reservation for attempting to lead their people in a new way of life. As bands of Lakota fled towards the camp of Red Cloud, one of the last surviving great leaders, they would be surrounded and massacred at a place called Wounded Knee.

CRAZY HORSE
RETRIBUTION SOCIETY

*O*n the same day that I received the
57-month sentence for aiding and abetting
the arson at MSU's fur animal research lab,
I also received another 57-month sentence for theft of government property for stealing
a five-by-seven inch book with a bullet hole through it. The book belonged to a Lt.
McIntosh of the US 7th Cavalry and the bullet hole came from a shot fired by a Lakota
warrior who was defending his family from an early morning ambush by military forces
led by General George Armstrong Custer at Greasy Grass, or the Battle of Little Bighorn.

In 1992 I visited the Greasy Grass battlefield to pay my respects to my fallen
indigenous brothers and sisters who had given their lives, past and present, to defend
Lakota sovereignty. I was outraged at the presentation of Custer's defeat as a great tragedy
committed by Lakota and Cheyenne "hostiles." There was no space on the battlefield
or in the adjacent museum to present the truth of the US government's violation of the
Fort Laramie Treaty of 1868 or the justifiable response of the indigenous peoples who
defended their families and way of life from sanctioned butchers. No grave markers
like those for the 7th Cavalrymen, detailing the many indigenous warriors who fell.

I decided to counter this disrespect of indigenous peoples who defended
their families and heritage with the theft of a Cavalryman's journal on
display, that was taken from a Lakota woman on the reservation by a soldier
distributing food rations. For stealing this over-glorified shopping list, I received
over four and a half years in prison while grave robbers and pot hunters on
indigenous lands, who desecrate the graves of our ancestors routinely, receive
probation. When I stole the journal I issued the following communiqué:

The Crazy Horse Retribution Society accepts responsibility for stealing Lt. McIntosh's
notebook from the battle monument. It was done to draw attention to the continued genocide
inflicted on Native American peoples and lands by the US government. Custer's defeat at
the Battle of Little Bighorn is describes at the battlefield museum as a tragedy. The real
tragedy is what lead native people to such drastic actions. Rape, mutilations, poverty,
religious persecution, and cultural assassination carried out by the 7th Cavalry continues
to this day by other US agents of repression on reservations across North America.

Misrepresentation of the struggle by Lakota, Cheyenne and Arapahoe to maintain their ancient traditions by fighting imperialist assimilation has forced native people today to take action. The desecration of native religion by the profane display of sacred objects in museums, and the destruction of sacred lands to mine uranium and coal for bombs and television is not conducive with the lessons of the Great Spirit. We demand equal representation at the battlefield in the form of displays and exhibits approved by the American Indian Movement. The explanation for the justified actions of Crazy Horse and Sitting Bull to defend their home and people at Little Bighorn is necessary before the notebook can be returned.

Until the US Government recognizes native sovereignty and suspends exploitive attitudes, teachings and behavior against the First Americans, we will rise up against the modern Custer's of US society.

AIM: A Founding Story

*E*ighty years after Wounded Knee, something began to happen as the restless spirits of those whose blood was spilled by the US began to fill the hearts of young Indian men and women in the 1970s. A resurgence had begun and the American Indian Movement was born. AIM warriors converged on the Lakota reservations at the invitation of the elders whose relations had fought and died against Custer on the Plains. Fighting tribal government corruption on the Pine Ridge rez, which sold uranium rich lands to the mining industry, AIM also began to rebuild traditional communities, bringing back the old ways to the youngsters of sweat lodges and sun dance ceremonies. AIM brought something to the reservations that the US government thought it had destroyed ages earlier. The memory of who we as indigenous people are, people with our own proud heritage of resistance and an identity with a culture that keeps our bond to mother earth alive.

Armed AIM militants at the Wounded Knee occupation, 1973

It wasn't long before corrupt officials and the US sent back in the cavalry. Launching a counter intelligence program, the FBI planted infiltrators, agent provocateurs and began a smear campaign against AIM's most vocal leaders. The FBI also supplied arms and ammunitions to AIM opponents who threatened, intimidated and murdered some of the Lakota's finest young traditional leaders. By 1980 over a hundred and fifty AIM members and supporters were dead with no investigation of their murders. Many also went to prison, such as Leonard Peltier who still sits in prison, charged with the killing of two FBI agents who, like Custer, had charged into a peaceful Lakota encampment with guns blazing.

Why the upside down flag? It is not meant as disrespect towards the very real sacrifices our elders made in defense of our freedom as US soldiers. Despite my personal opinions of war, I am grateful that my elders fought fascists such as Hitler, Mussolini, Franco and Tito in the Second World War. As early as the 1880's, Lakota delegations would fly the stars and stripes upside down to express their discontent over the

Mary Crow Dog, speaking at a demonstration, 1976

subhuman conditions on their reservations. When the Vietnam war ended and the many indigenous warriors who fought for the US returned to the rez, they not only found the same unwelcome as many other Vietnam veterans, but also a return to the subhuman treatment from the very nation they had been drafted to fight for. It was then, in the early 70s, that the American Indian Movement was spreading across the plains like a prairie fire. Many indigenous Vietnam veterans found within AIM an appreciation for their sacrifices and a much more dignified role as warriors for their own people.

Enlisted men and women are taught that a flag flown upside down is an internationally recognized symbol of distress and a state of emergency. Vietnam veterans within AIM could not deny that the conditions on Indian reservations were anything but a state of emergency.

The American flag represents the government of the occupying forces that have invaded North America. 220 years of colonization later and we are still fighting. In Northern Ireland the British have occupied the land since the 1100s and they are still fighting. Resisting occupational forces, indigenous peoples the world over are struggling to preserve their homelands, culture, language and basic human rights.

CANADA'S INDIAN WARS

"If this is civilization, then I'd rather be on the side of anarchy."
- Female Warrior of the Six Nations speaking about the 1990 military siege of Kahnesetake

*A*nd if you thought military intervention was something only the US utilized to break indigenous sovereignty in North America, think again. In the summer of 1995 the Defenders of the Shuswap Nation occupied the unceded lands of Gustafsen Lake in Alberta, Canada that by the Crown's own law is rightfully theirs. Following their annual sun dance ceremony, two dozen warriors from the Defenders established an encampment on the land and built a council house, declaring the area the heart of the sovereign government.

The Canadian State never entered into any treaty with the first nations of Western Canada, leaving all of British Columbia and portions of Alberta, such as Gustafsen Lake, unceded territories. By Crown Declaration of 1763, unceded territories and those lands that cannot be traced to a valid treaty remain indigenous lands.

The occupation of Gustafsen Lake met with the support of many Canadian bands of indigenous peoples, who for years have been struggling for the return of their stolen lands. The Canadian State responded to the occupation by calling in the cavalry. Regional police were dispatched to the area, and the Federal military provided armored personal carriers, one of which was disabled by Shuswap warriors. Land mines were also deployed surrounding the occupation site, which exploded underneath one of the warriors' vehicles while they were collecting water. When warriors fled the vehicle they were fired upon by police, wounding one of the warriors. The Defenders of the Shuswap Nation justifiably defended themselves from this second coming of the same armed and aggressive invaders by returning fire. Police forces prohibited all outside contact with the media or other supporters by jamming radio frequencies and cutting phone communications.

Indigenous mediators contributed to a peaceful settlement before police and military could kill or injure anyone else. Now the Defenders are in court facing serious charges such as attempted murder of law enforcement forces that illegally violated Shuswap sovereignty by laying siege to the unceded land at Gustafsen Lake.

Throughout Canada, indigenous resistance has been growing, with many native nations declaring themselves sovereign and blockading roads, bridges and railways across their lands. Indigenous warriors have also toppled power lines, burned bridges, sunk boats, destroyed logging equipment and been arrested defending their lands from government sanctioned corporate destruction. The Okanagan, Nuxalk, Tsilhot'in Nations, and the Haida band, have all declared themselves sovereign nations by right of Crow law, and have begun their fight to prevent the desecration of sacred lands and water, in some instances stopping military and logging exercises.

Not content to keep their promises to follow their own laws, the Canadian government has labeled any native band of sovereigntists that

Mohawk warrior patrolling barricade at Gustafsen Lake

fails to recognize their corrupt and illegitimate authority as extremists or terrorists. All in the same way that historically any independent indigenous community in the past was labeled hostile for not bowing to the authority of the occupational forces. Now the indigenous people of Canada, as wall as those of the US and Mexico, must face criminalization and imprisonment or death when simply defending their homelands, culture and people. And whoever said the indigenous nations of North America were defeated, when the Canadian, US and Mexican military are all presently engaged in actions to suppress native sovereignty and the rightful challenge for the return of stolen lands? From the rainforests of Western Canada to the jungles of Chiapas, indigenous peoples are rising up to reclaim what is theirs and to defend land, animals and people from the European descendants who would destroy them.

The Gustafsen Lake trail though still continuing is no longer news. Indigenous peoples taking up arms makes good newsprint, but those very same warriors defending their actions in court is of no interest to the mainstream media. Indigenous peoples of North America fighting for the return of their stolen lands is no competition for football players who kill their wives. It is up to indigenous peoples in the US and environmentalists everywhere to fight the very same injustice that threatens not only indigenous sovereignty but environmental protection as a whole. The First Americans are the only human civilization in North America which ahs proven successful to live in harmony with the land for thousands of years. It is time all others swallow their racial pride and listen to the voices that can save us all, rather than maintain our complacent silence while multinational corporations and North American governments and their militaries crush new generations of indigenous warriors. Our spirits cannot be broken. The spirit of our ancestors live within us. How many more must die before you realize the lives we are defending are also your own?

INTERNMENT CAMPS

Geronimo at the Fort Sam Houston internment camp. San Antonio, TX

*N*othing can convey to someone what prison is like if they've never been there before. It is not only about the physical conditions you are forced to endure; for me what is much greater is the psychological conditioning that one is subjected to. As a prisoner of war (I do not consider myself a political prisoner), I see my imprisonment as a modern-day equivalent of the outright murder of indigenous warriors in the last century. Though a state sanctioned death at the hands of "law enforcement" officers is a very real day-to-day threat for indigenous peoples, the risk of imprisonment or death skyrockets when one becomes "politically active." Especially when your activism is not confined to the avenues of what can be controlled by the government.

Geronimo was called a renegade in his day, even by some of his own people, because he refused to limit his protests to pleading with uncaring Indian Agents for enough food to survive on. His alternative was to work outside of the established system and create a dependency on the Earth that had sustained his people for generations. Of course, to the US government this was blatant lawlessness, and had they invented the word, I'm sure they would have called him a terrorist. For his "crimes" Geronimo and his people were held captive as prisoners of war longer than anyone else in US history.

In no way do I think I even come close to being half the man that Geronimo was, but I do feel a strong kinship with him and his resistance. As an indigenous person fighting for the preservation of mother earth, animals, indigenous peoples and our culture, my crimes are viewed as terrorism by the State. In the eyes of the Invader, my actions are all the more heinous because they were premeditated and targeted against industry. Here within the Bureau of Prisons this has earned me a "Public Safety Factor" which ensures that I will never do my time in anything less than a medium-security prison. It also ensures that I will not be awarded a furlough which I might otherwise be eligible for in this last two years of my sentence. Other than the PSF, I am the lowest security class inmate in the whole prison.

It is purely political that I have been given a PSF, as my sentencing judge originally recommended that I go to a prison camp or low security prison. In this way, I am treated very differently than other prisoners. I am one of the few prisoners who not only elected to come to prison as the consequences of engaging in activities I knew were illegal, but also I was unwilling to cooperate with the State in return for a shorter sentence, which is a common component in most federally prosecuted cases.

Like my ancestors who were sometimes outlaws simply because of the fact that they were forced to live under the laws of tyrannical society, I am an outlaw simply because I refuse to live by the laws that assert more rights to the inanimate property used to destroy life, than to the life that is being destroyed. Indigenous resistance in North America has always centered around the preservation of a worldview that asserts those rights to animals and the earth that the US *sometimes* asserts to human beings. The exception being if a human being is killed by military or law enforcement forces. Whether it be called indigenous worldview, animal rights or liberation, or biocentrism, it is all the same thing: the belief that what the Creator put here on this earth was for a purpose, a purpose that deserves respect and the right to free existence.

That is what I mean when I say that the psychological conditions of prison are much worse than the physical ones. To psychologically please my captors, who are also impacted by my crimes, I would have to renounce the very beliefs I and my ancestors lived by. Though I am a non-violent offender with virtually no record of violence in my life, my beliefs ensure that I will never be judged by my actual behavior in society, but more so by the laws I call into question because of their threats to the living earth and her animal people. In this way, to US eyes I will always be a terrorist and renegade.

Prison is like living in the midst of the dominating worldview, which sees animals as food, tools or entertainment; the earth as real estate, natural resources and private property; and humans as consumers, employees and sex objects. Prison reinforces the ideals that were first forced upon us when Columbus arrived in North America. Prisons are for all of those who have taken more than is allowed by the State, or for those who have fallen victim to the greed and quest for control and power that the government that imprisons them first encouraged.

As indigenous peoples we must see prisons as the internment camps for our warriors that our government has created and our communities neglect. As political activists we must view prisons as the punishment for those who refuse to obey the laws of our oppressors. And as human beings we should see prisons as evidence of the failure of the dominant worldview to provide justice, liberty and freedom to those people most persecuted and crushed by the powerful elite who now imprison them.

FOOD AS A
WEAPON

*L*ong before Columbus ever stumbled onto the beaches of North America, millions of indigenous peoples called this continent home. Many of these nations had developed regular trade routes across hundreds and even thousands of miles, and an agrarian society was maintained by many more. The typical stereotype of the indigenous North American is as the hunter, and though this is accurate for some indigenous nations, many cultures were not pushed towards a greater dependency on hunting until the arrival of Europeans who forced the indigenous populations away from sustainable agriculture and into a more nomadic existence.

The first English colonialist to land in what is now "New England" in the 17th Century wasted no time in capitalizing and literally stealing from the indigenous peoples' agricultural bounty. The Pilgrims who landed at Plymouth Rock record how they raided houses and storerooms of corn and other farmed foods and eventually through physical force took over already tilled lands rather than performing tedious task of clearing their own lands for cultivation. It is no secret that without indigenous people's assistance in learning how to grow their own food, the first European colonizers would have starved to death.

We can give thanks also to indigenous peoples' agrarian culture for such foods as corn, potatoes, many strains of bean and rice and a host of other plant foods that we sustain ourselves on today. In fact, more than half of all modern agriculturally produced crops were derived from plants domesticated by indigenous peoples. The historical denial of advanced agricultural methods practiced by indigenous nations is in keeping with the lies that we are not a highly civilized culture.

By labeling us as heathens (a term that described the pagans who lived on the heath, that is "wastelands" of Western Europe) and savages, the early colonists were able to justify the destruction of our societies without the concern one might give to the invasion and conquering of an already civilized land. Also, by denying advanced agricultural practices historians are able to continue the lie that the many millions of people that inhabited North America could not have existed as indigenous people were primarily "hunters and gathers." That is one of the biggest lies of the last 500 years.

Not only did we domesticate most of the food plants the western world eats today, but we also developed horticultural methods that created food surpluses that allowed peaceful trade with many other nations of indigenous peoples. Such facts speak the truth and are proof that North America was a highly populated civilization that was inhabited by tens of millions more people than is commonly taught or believed. Once the truth is known, the extent of European inflicted genocide becomes staggering to compare.

For indigenous people in the Southwest, hunting was a supplementary activity, overshadowed by horticultural practices which provided the basis of our food supply. For thousands of years indigenous peoples grew corn, beans and squash, which are called in some cultures, the "three sisters" because they were commonly grown together. It is believed that as many as 500 different varieties of corn were grown in the Americas previous to European conquest. Here in the Southwest, and in many other indigenous cultures, animals were not domesticated for food production, so no dairy products existed.

Previous to the Spanish Conquistadors' intrusion into the Southwest, many indigenous peoples sustained themselves on over 85% plant foods with very little animal protein. The Aqua Nation primarily was vegetarian with only occasional animal protein in the form of shellfish which were easily harvested from the sea. Nations that did sustain themselves on the killing of wildlife only did so after days of prayer and purification. Without a tremendous amount of preparation and respect the killing of an animal relation might bring unknown disaster to a people. The hunting of any animal was never tolerated for sport or for any reason but absolute necessity for survival. Our relationship with the animal world was a sacred one, and the death of an animal was seen a the death of a being on our own spiritual level.

Much changed when the Spanish arrived. The Spanish were quick to learn of our dependency on planted crops and began to burn farmlands and food stores as a way to create a greater dependency on their own rule. Nations living outside the control of the Spanish Crown were seen as a threat to Spanish colonization, especially because indigenous slaves immediately became necessary to the Spanish for their labor in the mines that produced the gold and silver necessary for the Spanish Kingdom to expand its empire through out the world. For the first time, many indigenous people who resisted this slavery and degradation were forced to hunt animals they rarely did before. For many nations, physical violence was also something they had rarely committed against humans.

It was during this time that the hunter and gatherer societies began in the Southwest on a large scale. The introduction of Spanish horses meant indigenous tribes could expand their range and compete for hunting lands, and the displacement of indigenous peoples from their homeland meant greater conflict with previously peaceful neighbors. Some indigenous peoples collaborated with the Spanish in exchange for their survival and for the first time large-scale warfare became common.

The Spanish were also responsible for the introduction of cattle, sheep and pigs into North America, thereby permanently altering many indigenous cultures such as the Navajo who began raising sheep for wool and meat. Other nations were forced into dependence on domestic livestock as their pre-conquest cultures were not possible during the centuries of armed struggle that began in the late 16th century. Commercial hunting near areas populated by Europeans depleted wildlife populations that in dire times provided sustenance for indigenous peoples during crop failures.

By the early 19th century many nations in the southwest were engaged in a lifestyle dependant on raids of neighboring tribes and European settlements which provided the food stores and supplies they were unable to raise and manufacture themselves. By the time non-Spanish Europeans reached the southwest in the 1800s, the face of Native America and subsequently the indigenous diet had been radically altered. As more and more indigenous peoples were dislocated from their native homelands, a greater dependancy on European trade was created. Periods of peace for many nations were infrequent enough to prevent the time necessary to till the land, plant, harvest and prepare food for storage.

As much as the war on indigenous peoples themselves was waged, so was the war on the indigenous way of life. Military installations were placed in the center of homelands and all indigenous peoples not under Spanish or American authority were often considered hostile. This forced those indigenous people resisting assimilitation further away from the peaceful pursuit of their pre-European lifestyle such as self-sustaining agriculture. By the time the 20th century rolled around, indigenous peoples found themselves surrounded by the rapidly increasing European and Mexican populations. Centuries of warfare eventually came to an end as the last indigenous nations laid down their arms.

Many nations were forced onto lands foreign to them that were often unsuitable for agriculture, the best farming lands going to the conquerors. A new way of life began for many who had never lived under the Euro-America rule. With their former lifestyle shattered, indigenous peoples were left with no alternative but to accept the meager handouts given to them by the US government. In Mexico, indigenous people were forced to work on large plantations growing cash crops such as coffee, henquen, sugar cane and corn that they would never eat themselves.

Here in Arizona, native people slowly lost touch with their agrarian heritage as they accepted livestock for their sustenance and began to create a dietary dependency on non-native foods. Gathering of wild foods and cultivation of crops was abandoned as native people entered the societal workforce where cash flow allowed them to obtain foods previously unavailable. Meat, dairy and processed foods high in sugar and cholesterol not only were purchased, but also continue to be provided by the US Department of Agriculture's commodity food program which often traffics food surpluses to indigenous peoples.

The metabolism and physiology of a people raised for thousands of years on wild and genetically unaltered plant foods in combination with unpolluted air and water has been severely affected by this foreign diet. Nutrition related health defects have been rampant on Indian Reservations. High rates of obesity, high blood pressure, diabetes and coronary disease are proof that the war on indigenous peoples continues on a different front. In the late 20th century, food is a weapon. The US has long used food aid as an incentive to break the will of indigenous people here and abroad.

Also, corporate agri-businesses have destroyed local and regional food production, ripped apart rural agrarian cultures, and pitted farmer against farmer as they struggle to survive in a world market dominated by corporations with a monopoly on the world's food supply. In many parts of North, Central and South America, indigenous peoples are economically blackmailed into growing corn and grain on lands that could feed their own families and villages. But due to their need to survive in a cash economy, they must provide the feed to the livestock industry.

All so the "First World" may have their Big Macs, Whoppers and other meat products that cost not only indigenous agrarian cultures, but also economically valuable land and water that could provide healthy foods in larger quantities to many poverty-stricken peoples. But all is not lost. A resurgence has began amongst indigenous peoples of the southwest as we rediscover the wild and agriculturally produced plant foods that not only provided sustenance for thousands of years, but also contribute greatly to lower levels of health problems.

Tepary beans, for instance, were grown here for hundreds of years and contain more protein than soybeans. Other wild plant food such has Prickly Pear have long been a food source for native people, and it is now known that the fruits and pads from the cactus are filled with vitamins and minerals and soluble fiber, which slows the absorption of sugars into the body, contributing to a reduction and even reversal of diabetes, which is common among native peoples of the southwest. A native plant-based diet similar to the one enjoyed by our ancestors also reduces cholesterol, which helps lower our risk of coronary heart disease.

Slowly, we are beginning to approach elders with knowledge of wild and traditional food plants to learn of the diet that can serve us. Also, from the Aqua Nation and other nations with people over the border in Mexico we are able to locate food plants that never disappeared from the diet of our relatives who never subscribed to the junk food culture. Some wild food plants have been found still surviving in isolated canyons and valleys where seeds might be harvested for the rebirth of our agrarian culture. Here in my desert homeland native foods include watermelon, sunflower seeds, corn, beans, squash, chilies, many varieties of cactus and a host of other wild and domesticated indigenous plant foods just waiting for rediscovery.

Since my return to the southwest a vegan diet has taken on a whole new meaning. It is not only a natural diet that provides optimum health, but also one that helps preserve a culture that was almost lost upon the introduction of commercial foods. Though not always vegan, our traditional diet can help our children learn the survival skills necessary to live self-sustainably, with little or no dependency on government handouts. By growing our own food we also return to a relationship with the earth that we have nearly lost in the world of fast-food and Safeways.

Harvesting wild plants also replaces us in the cycle of life, where it is easy to see the desert not as an inhospitable environment, but a world waiting to share with us the bounty that has sustained human and nonhuman life for generations. Though I have eaten animal products on rare occasion such as ceremonies and as a guest in impoverished households where any food is welcomed, I now consider it vital to demonstrate to my fellow people the benefit of a purely plant-based diet. Not only for our own health and that of the environment, but also in the hopes that it is possible now for us to return to the pre-conquest diet that let us live in a harmony with the animal world which we still know to be sacred.

The majority of our ceremonial foods have always been plant based: corn tamales, beans, squash, tortillas, flat enchiladas and chilies. It is not hard to remove the animal products from our diet without losing any of its cultural integrity. It is up to my generation to reintroduce the traditional diet that is not only one not dependant on corporate or government commercial foods both plant and animal, but also one that is available to those not able to afford the privilege of natural food stores and their overpriced products. A return to Native American Vegetarianism will always be a goal parallel to my desire for cultural preservation and protection of our homelands and sovereignty.

WHY I SUPPORT THE IRA

*W*hen we hear of Northern Ireland in the news it's usually in relation to the latest attack by the Irish Republican Army (IRA), but rarely if ever are we given the reasons behind what has now become 25 years of armed struggle. I myself fell victim to the media manipulation long ago and until recently felt justified in my criticism of the IRA's violent tactics– that is until I bothered to study a little Irish history of my own. What I discovered quickly erased the media brainwashing I had received in relation to the present day struggle in the north of Ireland. In no way can I do an 800 year old resistance to European colonialism justice in just a few pages, but what I hope to do is share my perception, as an indigenous person fighting

European colonialism in his own homeland, of the latest chapter in that resistance.

I chose to write about, in particular, the IRA hunger-strikes of 1981 because, as a prisoner held captive in one's own homeland for actions to defend her, I have a healthy amount of respect for prisoners of the same kind of war who are willing to give their lives for what they believed in. I also share the pain of anyone who has lost loved ones in the centuries-old resistance to a dominant power which has freely used legally sanctioned violence and terror to attempt to squash those who refuse to surrender their cultural identity and freedom.

When you begin to uncover the layer of lies that media and textbooks spread about the fight for Irish Independence, you begin to see a history of

1916

terrorism. But not one committed by the Irish Republican movement. You begin
to see violations of basic human rights that we are more familiar with Southeast
Asia, China, Central or South America. In Northern Ireland the last 25 years
have seen the British Government, especially its military operate with complete
impunity as they ruthlessly attempt to maintain control in their oldest colony.

The crisis in Northern Ireland has almost nothing to do with religion. It is not
the religious war between Catholics and Protestants that the media would have you
believe. It is the story of those who are loyal to the British Crown (Loyalists) and
in favor of Northern Ireland's continued union with Great Britain (Unionists); and
those who are fighting for Ireland as it once was, one nation one Republic, hence
the label Nationalists and Republicans. The last 800 years have seen many a British
invasion of the Emerald Isle, which in turn were met with many an Irish rebellion.

But, the greatest influence over Ireland's modern problems have been the result of British
military troops stationed in the six counties that make up Northern Ireland since 1970.

Previous to their arrival, the Royal Ulster Constabulary (RUC) went on the
rampage to crush the growing civil rights movement amongst the mostly Catholic
nationalist population. Inspired by the actions of Dr Martin Luther King, Jr in
America, Irish Nationalists began to organize for adequate housing and voting rights,
both of which had long been denied. The RUC's actions in 1969 were brutal. The
RUC (which to this day is 99% Protestant and 100% Loyalist) launched house to
house raids of suspected organizers smashing down front doors, arresting Irish citizens,
beating them viciously in the process and later torturing them. Paramilitary Loyalist
neighborhoods were given free reign to follow behind the RUC, burning out whole
neighborhoods of nationalists and sniping at the residents who fled their burning homes.

It was in this climate that the nationalist communities began to organize
barricades to protect their families and patrol against Loyalist attacks. Armed
only with rocks, sticks and crude Molotov cocktails, the nationalist communities
battled the RUC and the Loyalist gangs in the streets until the resulting riots led
to the deployment of British troops. By the summer of 1970, the British forces,
rather than protect the nationalist population, simply began to replace the RUC
as guardians of Loyalist rule and dominance. Nationalists responded by raining
bricks and bottles on British patrols who operated snatch squads that entered
barricaded communities to arrest Irish rioters. In acts of pure bravery, nationalists
would lure British soldiers down dead-end roads of then seal them off with with
barbed-wire. Nationalists would then rush out of their homes with hurling sticks
(used in a popular Irish sport) and engage the soldiers in hand to hand combat.

The more abusive and repressive the British became, the more politicized and
organized were the nationalist communities; women began patrols themselves,

following British soldiers through neighborhoods, verbally assaulting them for the violence they were committing against their families. In one Belfast neighborhood young people approached British soldiers and placed flowers in the barrels of their riffles. Still the Loyalists continued their attacks and fire bombings of homes and churches.

British forces announced a shoot-to-kill policy against rioting nationalists. It was in this climate of total urban chaos in the catholic neighborhoods of the North that the Irish Republican Army (IRA) that we know today re-emerged from their long slumber. With rusting antique weapons IRA volunteers took up sentry duty, awaiting Loyalist inclusions into nationalist zones where they made brave solitary stands against whole Loyalist mobs intent to burn them out of house and home. Many of these brave Irish warriors died protecting friends and family.

The British responded with total military occupational tactics: raiding homes in searches for arms and savagely beating whole families. Suspects were taken to military barracks where they were kicked, beaten and tortured.

Citizens began to be shot in the streets by rabid soldiers eager to intimidate the nationalist community. Internment was introduced in 1970 and six month sentences handed out for "disorderly behavior." The Loyalist attacks continued, as did nationalist riots with Loyalist and British soldiers. By mid-1971 the IRA had carried out 125 retaliatory bombings within two months. The British responded with a shoot-to-kill policy of any males of "military age." In what were little more than hunting expeditions, British soldiers began shooting innocent Irish citizens and firing and killing any community members who tried to aid wounded friends.

In spite of this brutal repression, the civil rights struggle continued. Loyalists responded by bombing public buildings and assassinating activists. The attacks on peaceful protests reached a head when in January of 1972 British troops opened fire on 20,000 marchers, killing thirteen and wounding those who tried to save their fallen comrades.

The following day the press reported that the IRA had launched an attack on the army post and that five "terrorist gunmen" had been shot. All of this activity led to massive recruitment for the republican cause. Where many residents had been previously opposed to armed struggle, many now saw it as the only means left to protect their families. Far from protecting Irish citizens, the British occupational forces had joined the RUC and the Loyalists in waging a bloody war against the nationalist movement.

By July British snipers were literally executing citizens in their own neighborhoods. In one attack, a 13 year-old girl was shot; in another neighborhood a priest and another man were shot and killed coming to the aid of teens who also had been shot by the same British snipers. A brave 15-year old tried to reach the priest and other victims and was shot eight times. The IRA arrived later on the

1974

International women's day 1982

INLA poster marking March 8th, International Women's Day. the caption originally read: This is not a men's war, it is a people's war!

scene and began to direct gunfire at the sniper position while one survivor was evacuated.

By 1981 the situation in Northern Ireland had turned the six counties into a war zone. Responding to the resilient persistence of the IRA who refused to surrender their homelands and communities to the imperialist rule of British invaders, the government had removed special category status for prisoners that had previously been recognized as political internees. Over 3,000 Irish citizens found themselves in British jails and prisons for opposing the occupation. Meanwhile Loyalist paramilitary groups, many of whom were made up of off-duty RUC officers and British soldiers, continued their campaigns of violence and terrorism.

It was in this atmosphere that IRA prisoners continued their resistance from behind bars. Since the suspension of political status for the Prisoners of War (POWs), convicted IRA members had began "blanket protests" where they refused to wear prison uniforms, opting to wrap themselves in blankets instead. This resulted in punishments and abuse from prison authorities which led to "no-wash protests" as the blanket protesters were refused shower privileges.

The blanket protests had continued for over four years with no indication from the British State that a settlement was in sight, nor had the British made any effort to negotiate. IRA prisoners intended to escalate their protests by embarking on hunger-strikes that had earlier in the 70s succeeded in winning the political status that was recently removed. The hunger strike had long been a weapon of Irish nationalists, dating back to feudal times when it was used to force the settlement of grievances with British lords and kings. It had also been used in the early 1900s by Irish nationalists that hunger-striked to death.

THE HUNGER STRIKE

"Our revenge will be the laughter of our children"

Bobby Sands

It wasn't until the repression of the 1970s that hunger-striking returned to the republican cause. In June 1972, 40 IRA prisoners went on strike demanding official prisoners of war status. After 37 days the British granted "special" status as part of a deal that also led to a short-lived cease-fire. The removal of this status in 1976 led to the blanket protests and hunger-strike of 1981. Along with the criminalization of the Irish Republican struggle by Prime Minister Margaret Thatcher that began in 1976 also came a propaganda campaign that continues to ignore the brutal police and military repression in Northern Ireland today.

In the early 1970s, Irish Republicans were interned in derelict World War Two British Army bases. As the imprisonment of activists and IRA volunteers increased alongside their resistance, the British State responded by building a maximum-security prison that could be totally surrounded and patrolled by the British Army.

Irish prisoners in the H-block (named after the shape of each cell-block) maintained a system of organization that recognized their military structure within the IRA. Officer Commanders were chosen by the outside IRA army council, and these prisoners ensured that grievances and demands of the POW's were heard. Morale amongst IRA prisoners was such that in republican H-Blocks lectures were organized on politics, Irish history, religion and the Irish language. Prisoners in a less formal atmosphere also performed sing-along sessions, story telling and poetry readings.

On February 5th, the commanding officer announced the beginning of a hunger-strike that would eventually end with the death of ten strikers. The demands centered on political status which allowed them exemptions from wearing prison uniforms and from forced labor, allowed freedom of association, improved mail and visits, and replacement of lost time-off their sentences as a result of the blanket protests.

The first to begin the hunger-strike was a 27 year-old man named Bobby Sands. For Sands the struggle against the British occupation began in his teens in the early 70s, as he watched his neighborhood go up in flames. Many of his friends and family members were killed by British troops. Joining the IRA at 18, he was captured a month later and sentenced to three years in Long Kesh, the internment camp.

There he learned Irish and became very interested and active in political lectures given by some of the most liberated Irish republicans at the time. Bobby was also a fabulous musician and song writer, often entertaining his fellow prisoners. Released in 1976, he immediately began organizing political meetings and social events for teens, and editing a community paper called *Liberty*. He sang songs of Irish freedom and rejoined the IRA.

He was arrested and given a 14 year sentence for possession of a single revolver.

Upon his arrival in the new Long Kesh H-Blocks, he joined the blanket protest and continued his political writings as well as teaching the Irish language. It is said that if you borrowed a book from Bobby, upon its return he would quiz you on it, and, failing to provide satisfactory answers, he would send you back to read it again. He served as Officer Commander on an early hunger-strike that failed to achieve results, so when the February strike began he was a natural volunteer candidate.

Bik McFarlance replaced Sands as OC, and Bobby refused his first meal on March 1, 1981, the anniversary of phasing-out political status. Bobby had written earlier, "An armed people are by no means a sure guarantee to liberation. Our guns may kill our enemies, but unless we direct them with the politics of a revolutionary people they will eventually kill ourselves." After the death of the Minister of Parliament for the Fermanagh/South Tyrone district, a by-election was called to replace him.

Sinn Fein, the political wing of the IRA, had yet to establish the revolutionary politics Sand had earlier written of, and now was their chance. Sands was nominated and Sinn Fein began to feverishly campaign for Bobby, who represented not only the republican struggle, but the demands of political prisoners.

Since her election to British Prime Minister, Margaret Thatcher had begun a criminalization policy in Northern Ireland, whereby the IRA was portrayed as armed thugs and terrorists with no support in their home country. Through trials without juries and broad judicial powers, Thatcher was quickly filling British prisons with the IRA's mostly young recruits, who stood almost no chance of being acquitted once targeted and arrested by British forces. Now these very same young warriors were given the chance to prove Thatcher wrong.

In less than one month, 30,000 Irish registered their support for Sands and the hunger-strike and elected him Minister of Parliament, much to Thatcher's disgust. Though he would never fill his seat in the British Parliament, Sinn Fein and the IRA had proven wide support for the struggle to free Ireland from British occupation. The victory was short-lived. Thatcher continued to ignore the demands of the hunger-strikers and refused to recognize Sands as a legitimate Member of Parliament. On May 5th, Bobby died after 66 days without food.

Sands' body was returned home where over 100,000 mourners lined the funeral routes. Protests and marches in support of the hunger-strike and Sands took place in the US, Poland, Portugal, France, Switzerland, West Germany, Belgium, Holland, Greece, Italy, Australia and Norway. The city of Tehran, Iran renamed the street where the British embassy is located Bobby Sands Street.

Thatcher refused to budge, despite the pleadings and condemnations from some world governments urging her to negotiate with the strikers. Sands' death not only set off riots and retaliatory action against the British government because of its refusal to even consider the demands, it also galvanized the hunger-strikers' commitment to achieve victory.

Francis Hughes was a 25 year-old republican who had joined the IRA when he was 16 after watching his older brother dragged away out of the family house to internment camps. Hughes became a living legend amongst the IRA by the time he was 22. The British estimate that as many as thirty soldiers and policemen died at his hands. As one senior IRA commander stated, "He was the sort of man who would shoot up a few policemen on his way to a meeting to plan our next attack on the police."

By 1978, he was Northern Ireland's most wanted man when he was captured in a shootout with a British Army patrol. Sentenced to life imprisonment plus 20 years, Hughes began his hunger-strike two weeks after Sands.

There were still no signs of government willingness to negotiate. The hunger-strike's strategy was to pressure the British government into an embarrassing situation in the media, where their failure to negotiate a deal would be seen as callous and inhumane. Though the deaths of four hunger-strikers had ignited high emotion in the Irish and even parts of the international community, it failed to force the government to the table. Thatcher believed that any consideration of the prisoner's demands was tantamount to negotiating with terrorists. She blatantly referred to the hunger-strikers as murderers, failing to recognize that the IRA was no different from their ancestors who, for 800 years, have fought against British colonialism with an equally defensive zeal. It was all a part of the criminalization policy which sought to change peoples' minds about the struggle in Northern Ireland from a political and military occupation to an "anti-terrorism" campaign.

In Dublin, the capitol of the Irish Republic, elections were called for June 11. Once again the republican community mustered their new-found political savvy and ran nine prisoners for office, four of them hunger-strikers. Running on the platform of supporting the republican prisoners' five demands two hunger-strikers, Kieran Doherty and Paddy Agnew, were elected. A third, Joe McDonnell, came within 300 votes of winning and was the sickest of the strikers. During this stage of the protests the British Foreign Office began secret negotiations with Sinn Fein on the condition that there be no public knowledge of them. But in the midst of negotiations, the British pulled out and it was later learned that McDonnell had died July 8th.

Joe McDonnell's son had once drawn a picture of his father snatching the keys from a guard and opening all the cells. The text accompanying it said, "And now all the daddies are home with their children..."

Joe, the oldest of the strikers at 30, was a close friend of Sands, and had been arrested with him. He was buried next to his old friend and comrade-in-arms, Fianna Eireann, who was shot by the British Army on July 10th. At Joe McDonnell's funeral the RUC attacked the procession in an attempt to arrest the IRA honor guard. In the melee one mourner was shot in the back. Another mourner informed the masses that Daniel Barrest, another 15 year-old, had been shot and murdered by British troops. A former IRA Chief of Staff told a crowd of mourners, "The British government understands only one thing: force."

Indeed, just before McDonnell's death the British Parliament had passed a new law preventing prisoners from running for Parliament as Sands had, thereby sealing off one of the few avenues of democracy available to Irish republicans. Thatcher continued to accuse the IRA of forcing the deaths of its prisoners, and a documentary on the hunger-strikers was censored as republican propaganda because it showed Patsy O'Hara in his coffin. Once again the British establishment was suppressing rebel voices from Northern Ireland, as the prisoners support group was also prohibited from broadcasting interviews with the "extremists."

Martin Hurson was arrested when he was 22 for attempting to blow up British troop vehicles and sentenced to 20 years. By the time he joined the hunger-strike he had spent five years in prison. After 46 days on strike, Hurson died on July 13th.

25 year-old Kevin Lynch joined the IRA when he was 15, later joining the Irish National Liberation Army (INLA), another armed resistance group, when he was 20. He was arrested a year later and sentenced to ten years, and, like many of the other strikers, he had been part of the blanket protest.

Joining Kevin on his strike was Kieran Doherty who had early won the election in Dublin. He joined the youth brigade of the IRA when he was 16, spent two and a half years in internment camps when he was 17, and was later arrested for a bombing when he was 20.

Kieran came from a long line of republican warriors, many of his family members having been killed in action. With six men already dead, Sinn Fein's head, Gerry Adams, visited the strikers as a voice for the movement to express support for any decision they might make. "Any individual could call off their own strike; they could compromise the five demands or continue." Whatever the case, Adams wanted to make it clear that the decision rested with the hunger-strikers, not the Army Council or anyone else. Doherty responded, "We haven't got our five demands and that's the only way I'm coming off. Too many suffered for too long, too many good men dead. Thatcher can't break us. I'm not a criminal. For too long our people have been broken… We won't be broken. We'll get our five demands. If I'm dead… well, the others will have them. I don't want to die, but that's up to the Brits. They think they can break us. Well they can't. Tiocfaidh ar la (Our day will come)."

On August 1st, Kevin Lynch died after 71 days on hunger-strike, and Kieran followed after 73 days. Within an hour of Kieran's death, the IRA launched a rocket attack on British armored vehicles; earlier in the day two policemen were killed when an IRA unit triggered a 600 pound bomb under their car.

Following Lynch and Doherty's death Bik McFarlane, the commanding officer for the hunger-strikers and their chosen representative, conducted a poll amongst the republican prisoners. 30% wanted to call a halt to the protest; another 30% didn't think they would win. The remaining 40% demanded a no compromise stance. Police also released figures on the violence accompanying the hunger-strike: 51 dead, 10 policemen, 13 soldiers, over 1,000 injured and 1,700 arrested.

23 year-old Tom McElween died on August 8th after a 62-day strike. At his funeral a Sinn Fein official said, "We do not claim to be perfect, nor do we claim the certainty of God's blessing on our work. But we stand over this, that as sure as there's a sun in the sky and as the earth turns on its axis, then there can never

be moral wrong in an oppressed people using force against their oppressors."
The week also marked the ten-year anniversary of interment, whereby republicans
could be imprisoned without trial. It was estimated that over 1,000 firebombs were
thrown in ensuing riots, while two republicans were killed. One by a plastic bullet
and the other, a 16 year-old boy, shot by a passing car as he walked with friends.
Mickey Devine was 14 when he began throwing rocks at the British troops.
When he was 18 he joined the IRA. He was among the marchers who were
gunned down by British troops on Bloody Sunday. When he was 20 he left the
IRA and helped found the INLA. The following year he was captured in an
arms raid and sentenced to 12 years where he immediately joined the blanket
protest. On June 22 he began his hunger-strike and on August 20th, after 66
days, he died. Mickey would be the last to die in the nationalist hunger strikes of
1981. In August family intervention had brought the end of the hunger-strikes.

Far from being a failure, the hunger-strike gave the Irish republican
movement international attention and allowed the struggle to prove its
support, even politically, by the election of Sands and other hunger-strikers.

*Though Northern Ireland is still in the control of the British State, the IRA signed a peace agreement in
1998 that has produced a lasting cease-fire. In the summer of 2005 the IRA officially began to disarm.*

BOOK TWO
MEMORIES OF FREEDOM

*"A single act of defiance is worth
more than a thousand angry words."*

CHAPTER ONE
Take No Prisoners

*S*itting around the campfire one night, some of us warriors of the Animal Liberation Front decided it was time we say a few words about our deeds as continually we are labeled by those outside of our circle as everything except what we are: Terrorists, Extremists, Fanatics, Doctors, Lawyers?, "Animal Rights Activists". Sure there have been cells who might fit some of those descriptions, but not us. Since few people ever see our communiques except the corporate-controlled media, few would understand that our concerns go way beyond animal abuse. In our view from the shore, we see animal abuse as just one symptom of a much larger disease. That disease, which also brings us racism, sexism, militarism, environmental destruction, alcoholism, drug abuse, domestic violence, male domination and a downright bad attitude toward our fellow creation, just to name a few. What has caused us to be plagued with these diseases when the world we are given could be such a beautiful place? That's not for us to discuss. We're warriors, not philosophers. Whatever it is, we see that disease slowly creeping into our various struggles and it makes us want to cry. Rumors, back-biting, inflated egos, trying to get laid, trying to raise funds by appearing "respectable", we've all seen it and it's causing our movement to self-destruct, just as they begin to become truly the catalyst for real change.

Now we're far from perfect ourselves; we have made our mistakes, hurt each other, but from where we stand we are far from giving up. We don't want to see others make the same mistakes we have made, hence this 'zine. This is a story. The story of a handful of people who cared enough to risk their lives and freedom for what they believe. For Earth and for the release of the prisoners of the war on nature. It hasn't been without its costs. Though we are all here tonight, one of us is sitting in an 11 by 7 foot cell in Federal Prison for the next four years. He isn't the first and he sure as hell won't be the last. In this story there are many chapters. We are but one. The rest is up to you. We are here to tell you about our moments of victory and defeat. Our moments of tremendous joy at being alive on this beautiful planet earth as we fought proudly in her defense, and our moments of great despair when the whole world seemed against us.

Mostly this 'zine is about a struggle that began before our great grandparents were alive. It's about a spirit. The spirit of freedom and the spirit of the wild that refuses to be tamed. It's about a struggle that began long before the term "Animal Rights" was ever spoken. When Earth First! wasn't a slogan, but a way of life… and death. It's about remembering the past and remembering that those of us who choose to represent the Earth Mother and her Animal Nations now inherit a responsibility that others have been killed fulfilling and which we must put before anything else in our lives, including our own freedom if necessary. It's about power. Not manmade power, but the power that only the spirit of Earth can give us. The power we receive when we awaken to the sounds of the coyotes song, and the howling wind through the last ancient old-growth trees. Power that no man can give us and power that no man can take away. Power that can lift us above our enemies to become the type of warriors we only hear about in myths and legends. Power that is just waiting for us to rediscover and unleash. It is about breaking the chains wrapped around us beginning on that first day of school, the first day of work. Chains that slowly wrap around us until we are ready to be considered responsible adults, but because of those chains we have forgotten how to move, how to be free, how to live in harmony with all of life, with the four-leggeds, the winged ones and all the animal people as our brothers and sisters.

Let's face it, many of us are afraid. Afraid of being wrong. Afraid of being alone. Afraid of spending years on prison. Afraid of being shot or incinerated, like 60 adults and 24 children in Waco, Texas at the bloody hands of the u.s. Government. Fear is our enemy's greatest weapon because unlike having to place a police officer in every home, it is already there, waiting to be unleashed with carefully orchestrated images on corporate controlled t.v. and newspapers. Prison cells with their iron doors slamming shut, police beatings by baton-wielding Nazis, "terrorists" being led away in orange suits and chains, images that keep our fear at being different alive and strong.

The Plains Indians have a saying they would yell going into battle, "Hoka Hey!" It is a good day to die! To us, that meant they had overcome that most common of fears, that fear of death. Unleashed from their fears of death, they would charge forward into battle against people who were very much afraid to die and as a result, those warriors won the only victory in which an unconditional surrender was signed by the US Government, in its history, Red Clouds War of the 1860's. Much like those of us who would rather die than live in a world without wilderness and animals, those brave warriors overcame their fears of imprisonment and death because they knew the power of the Earth was very real. Not just a belief, but a reality. Much more real than anything the u.s. Government had to offer. A reality where all animals were messengers and every mountain a cathedral. The stories we read about those tribes and their relationship with the Earth, Animals and their spirits, were not myth or folklore, they were and are real. Real enough to drive a human to sacrifice all in their world for the hope that future generations might share in that same power that lies within the spirit of every living being and flows through every wild creation. For the hope that you, the children of earth might awake to the screams of our tortured earth and her animal people. It is over 100 years since the true Warriors of the Earth gave their lives on this continent for the Earth Spirits and Animal People. Through the years, often the spirits of resistance have arisen, always to be beaten back by prisons and bullets, lies and deceit. Now it is your turn. Whether you realize it or not the spirit of all those fallen warriors are watching. Watching to see if you will rediscover the power that the Animal People and their wilderness homes can give us. The power that breaks our chains and awakens our spirit to the realization, that you represent possibly, the last hope for this planet we all call home.

There are those who can see the horrors of vivisection and fur farming. The oil covered shorelines and the clearcut mountainsides, and plod forward through the muck of lobbying, petitioning, letter-writing, politicking and protesting. This 'zine is not for them. This 'zine is for every young man and woman who has cried for the blood of the Earth, stood in shock, open-mouthed at the callousness and cruelty some can inflict on our peacefullest of fellow creations, the Animal People. For everyone who has ever felt helpless against an enemy a thousand times larger than yourself.

For those who cannot live with the pain of knowing that every morning the laboratory lights are turned on, the chainsaws are oiled and sharpened, the gas chambers are wheeled out to the pelting barns, and the slaughter is continuing, this is for you, so that you may never feel alone again, so that you may see that though we may never achieve total victory in our lifetimes, sometimes victory and freedom is ours simply by fighting, by breaking our own chains before we can break the chains of others.

For you we speak out and tell the story of what a handful of warriors can do, what a handful of warriors must do. A handful of people just like you.

CHAPTER TWO
The Radical Environmental Movement in America

In the 1980's much was happening to the previously mild environmental and animal rights movements in America. These movements had primarily been occupied with tactics ranging from petitioning, letter-writing, boycotts, lobbying, public-awareness campaigns and on the extreme, protests and civil disobedience. Reagan-era politics meant few victories in the fight to protect wilderness and animals despite the fact that animal issues have generated more mail to Washington D.C. than any other topic, including the Vietnam War. The earth-raping policies of James Watts' Interior Department were some of the catalysts that brought rise to Earth First! and the phrase No Compromise In Defense of Mother Earth! For the first time in almost 100 years an organized resistance was born on behalf of wilderness and wildlife. Unfurling a huge "crack" across the face of Glen Canyon Dam, the dam that tamed the wild Colorado River, Earth First!ers declared themselves the modern day warriors of the environmental movement. One of the Earth First! movements first actions was the erection of a monument to Victorio, a Mimbes Apache leader who had attacked mining operations and camps in his quest for the liberation of his land and people. Though controversial in the modern West, the best was yet to come. One of the greatest tactics resurrected from indigenous resistance was the act of monkey wrenching which Earth First! openly spoke of, and advocated, that is the destruction of machinery and equipment being used to defile the earth and her wild places. Timber sales had trees spiked with long nails intended to deter sawmills from wanting to process the trees. Bulldozers were the target of mechanical sabotage as were other pieces of heavy equipment. Roads into critical wildlife habitat were spiked with intent to puncture tires of offending vehicles. Billboards began to fall across the West and survey stakes with their blaze orange tape were ripped from the earth at development sites.

Suddenly, when legitimate protests failed to protect a wilderness area, activists no longer felt helpless as the bulldozers rolled near, or the chainsaws began to roar. Monkeywrenchers began to roam the west once more, leaving in their path incinerated and sabotaged mining and logging equipment along with spiked timber sales. The profit margin of earth destruction was narrowed as loggers, developers and road builders had to factor in the potential for sabotage. This meant increased security and high insurance premiums, all of which cut into the earth rapists' profit margin. "Eco-Defense: A Field Guide To Monkeywrenching" by Dave Foreman became the bible of every earth warrior fed up with the ineffectiveness of legitimate protest, and served as a "how-to" manual for would-be saboteurs. In the West where Earth First! and monkeywrenching was the most prevalent, other activists who shared many of Earth First!'s sentiments began to see how those tactics could benefit animal liberations, as well as preservation. As the frustration of ineffectiveness and compromise were common place in both movements. The warriors of Earth began to awake from their long slumber.

CHAPTER THREE
The Animal Rights Movement in America

At the same time Earth First! and monkeywrenching surfaced in the US, the animal rights movement in America began to employ a tactic that had originated in Britain. Breaking into animal research laboratories, rescuing the animals used in experiments and damaging the equipment used to conduct experimentation. Borrowing the name of an underground group in operation in the U.K. since the 1970's, the Animal Liberation Front was born in the United States. More animals are killed in the U.S. for food, fur, research purposes and wildlife control than in any other country. After years of fighting legal battles to reduce the slaughter, with little or no effect, an avenue of action was born and activists rejoiced in the sight of videos released by the ALF depicting hooded members smashing down doors to enter animal labs and spiriting away the animals to freedom. The ALF brought a breath of fresh air to a previously stifling movement that rarely rocked the institutions of animal abuse it opposed.

Suddenly many American activists found themselves debating the pros and cons of breaking the law on behalf of animals. Mainstream animal rights groups began to weigh the potential loss of revenue generated by supporting illegal activity and possible loss of public support for animal rights, a belief in itself that was radical to most members of American society, with the ALF scene as the "extremist fringe". While others quibbled with the blatant questioning of the authority of the U.S's self serving corporate protecting laws, others had little doubt that what the ALF achieved was having an effect on the animal abuse industry like never before.

Until 1987, the ALF had only engaged in animal liberation activities with destruction of research equipment limited to what could be accomplished in the few minutes during the raids. In one raid of animal research labs at the University of Pennsylvania, videotapes stolen by the ALF of the researchers callousness towards baboons filmed by the researchers themselves, was later used to help shutdown that laboratory.

Other targets of the ALF were effected with research funds being cut-off. But in most cases animals were replaced, security measures at research labs increased, and the experiments continued with a greater realization by vivisectors that some actions in the animal rights movement could not be controlled or predicted. Though ALF liberations meant salvation for the animals rescued, ALF activists questioned whether the animal abuse industries were being affected as much as possible. If the ALF ever intended to put animal abusers out of business for good in America, other tactics would have to be employed. Tactics which struck at the very center of their cold hearts, in their profit margin. Once again a view across the eastern ocean held the answer.

CHAPTER FOUR
This is the A.L.F.! The Youth Take Charge...

In the late April evening of a warm California night ALF warriors jumped a chain-link fence on the campus of the University of California at Davis and changed the face of the animal rights movement in America forever. The next morning a state of the art animal diagnostic research laboratory would be a smoldering ruin, the victim of an arson attack that left no injuries and $3 million in damage. It would be over a year before the lab would recover from the attack and open its doors. Never before had the ALF employed arson in the U.S., while in Britain it was already an accepted tactic. For the first time in the history of the U.S. animal rights movement, an animal research laboratory was destroyed before it even opened. Federal investigators rushed to the scene and suddenly, the animal rights movement became a target of investigation. Animal rights activists unfamiliar with the accomplishment of something in one night that couldn't be achieved with years of legal activism, were quick to distance themselves from the UC-Davis fire and other ALF type actions and began to condemn the ALF. For many in the animal rights movement, their struggle was about reforming cruel practices, not abolishing the institutions which perpetuated commercial animal exploitation. The UC-Davis fire was the product of much discussion amongst the strategists of the ALF. Would the ALF maintain its Robin Hood persona, whisking animals to freedom with much public support, or would they launch a campaign of economic sabotage intent on costing animal abusers millions in expensive security improvements and increased insurance premiums as well as maximum property destruction. Already the ALF was known to launch small "smash attacks" against fur shops and fast-food eateries. Breaking windows with bricks and slingshots and sloganing with signature blood red spray paint. The decision was a strategic one. Public support was nice, but alone it had rarely saved animals lives. All those letters to Washington DC wastepaper baskets were proof of this. The industries of earth destruction and animal abuse were firmly favored by the U.S. political structure and never would politicians enact and enforce laws that cost them the financial support of big businesses that put them in office. The campaign of maximum destruction, not minimum damage to the equipment of animal abusers had begun, and with it came a new element of the animal rights movement never before seen in the U.S.

Often ALF actions were signed with the trademark "ALF" in red paint, but in Davis, the circle "A", anarchy symbol was affixed to the "A" of the ALF's signature. To those who bothered to look beneath the carefully controlled media coverage of ALF actions this was a sign that the ALF was no longer simply just an "animal" group but one that also was opposed to the entire system which perpetuated animal abuse. Press releases following ALF actions after 1987 often drew connections to animal abuse and environmental destruction and human liberation. The anarchistic influence in the ALF also was proof that the ALF saw through the facade of the "first world" to the underlying corruption of the U.S. political process.

The ALF no longer was only opposed to society's mistreatment of animals, but also the institutions that thrived on human abuse and control, environmental degradation and the impact first world business practices had on members of poverty-stricken indigenous peoples the world over, who provided America with the fat of their land. The lines between animal rights and animal liberation had become clearly drawn. No longer would the ALF only represent the predominantly upper-middle class majority who most represented the animal rights movement. ALF actions began to reflect the frustration and oppression felt by various members of America's citizens who like the animals were victimized by big business first and everything else last. In less than two months of the UC-Davis fire the Western Wildlife Unit of the ALF was formed to deal specifically with the war on America's wildlife. Their first action occurred on Memorial Day, 1987 when over 200 wild horses were re-released into their homeland range in Northeastern California where they were being removed to make room for cattle grazing operations. Already in the West livestock comprised over 70% of available grazing land and wild horses meager 2%, yet they were seen as competition with the politically powerful cattlemen's lobby. In a policy supported by many animal welfare groups, the horses are rounded up and slated for adoption, never again to roam free on America's landscape as they have for over 400 years. Immediately following the wild horse liberation, the Western Wildlife Unit visited UC-Davis, this time releasing three turkey vultures used in poison studies for the deadly tool of the U.S. Department of Agriculture Animal Damage Control programs; compound 1080, a poison most frequently used to kill small mammals and predators living on lands grazed by livestock. 1987 ended with the rescue of four beagles used in studies of the effects of air pollution from the University of California at Irvine by the ALF. Such research was the epitome of not only our treatment of animals but also our irresponsibility in protecting our environment. The bridge between animal abuse and environmental destruction was beginning to cross the gap that had previously existed between radical environmentalists and animal liberationists. Apparently it was not a one way effort. In 1988 an Earth First! offshoot claimed responsibility for an attempted firebombing of the California Cattlemens Association offices in Sacramento and the near total destruction of a livestock auction yard in nearby Dixon. In 1988 there were more ALF actions and instances of Earth First! Inspired monkeywrenching than in any previous year recorded in the U.S. The struggle continued with lab raids across the country culminating in the largest raid on an animal research laboratory in the United States. In April, 1989 the ALF simultaneously broke into four separate animal research labs and offices at the University of Arizona in Tucson destroying one laboratory with fire, causing irreparable damage to computer records at animal research offices with fire in a separate administrative office, as well as rescuing 1,200 mice, rats, rabbits, guinea pigs and frogs from vivisection labs on campus. 1989 ended with not only a full-force investigation of animal rights groups by federal authorities, but a sting operation against Earth First! that netted four activists attempting to topple powerlines in the Arizona desert. The sting revealed that one of the monkeywrenchers was actually an FBI agent who had infiltrated the warriors' circle for two years.

In 1990 powerlines were toppled on Earth Day in Watsonville, CA, to dramatize the dependence on coal and oil burning power-plants which fed on indigenous peoples' lands and contributed to carbon dioxide emissions. This action was later allegedly connected to the Animal Liberation Front. Following the "Earth Night Action Group's" power outage, Earth First! organizers were the victims of a car-bomb that seriously wounded one of the activists. The FBI was quick to arrest the bombing victims, accusing them of transporting explosives, while no investigation was launched into death threats previously received by the Earth First! organizers, allegedly from individuals within the timber industry. Truly the 1990's would see a raising of the stakes in defense of Mother Earth and her Animal Nations. As the FBI hunted warriors for the earth and animal liberation, people began to realize that this was a struggle that yet again could end in death or imprisonment for its participants.

Within the ALF, divisions began to develop, not just over arson but about media and euthanasia. Sadly enough, some ALF cells believed in killing healthy animals once rescued, rather than risk finding safe homes for them. Already arguments had erupted in the midst of ALF actions between activists who wanted to dump animals rather than carry them away when alarms were triggered or when homes could not be found. In an ALF raid at the University of Oregon in 1986, eight laboratory rabbits were recovered by vivisectors after having been dumped near a road not far from the labs. It began to be apparent that some ALF activists were more concerned with media coverage and acknowledgement of their actions than the animals' lives themselves. On Independence Day 1990, the ALF rescued 100 guinea pigs from Simonsen Laboratories in California only to have some activists advocate dumping the animals when homes could not be found. This resulted in a further split, within the ALF as the pro-life ALFers took the guinea pigs and spent many weeks finding them safe homes. Meanwhile the youthful element of the ALF began to be known in the ALF network as "pro-lifers" because of their refusal to kill healthy animals rescued from laboratories and factory farms. These names were being given by ALF activists who regularly euthanised healthy animals rescued from labs while their press releases claimed they had been delivered to safe homes. Most of these media orientated activists also believed that arson was a tactic that cost public support and drew undue police repression. The Western Wildlife Unit, anarchist cells and youth brigades of the ALF argued that police repression was only proof that through illegal direct action, especially arson, the ALF had seriously begun to breed fear amongst animal abusers not to mention inflict more damage to labs, factory farms and other institutions than strictly animal liberation raids ever had. Young voices also came forward and pronounced that if the ALF had begun to justify violence against animals, who could be truly counted on to stop it? For them and us, liberation meant freedom from a certain death at the hands of humans, be them vivisectors, factory farmers, or media-hungry animal rights activists. The responsibility of the animal liberator did not end when the laboratory was destroyed, but when all of its prisoners were guaranteed sanctuary in safe homes or returned to their native habitat.

CHAPTER FIVE
Fur Farming in America

As 1990 came to a close, the ALF grew silent as its members struggled with strategic and ethical differences, as well as ever present FBI investigators hounding suspected activists. During this time news began to surface within the animal liberation movement of an investigation of America's fur farms. In early 1991 videos began to circulate of mink farmers brutally breaking the necks of mink with their bare hands and of bobcats and lynx pacing neurotically in tiny cramped cages four foot square. One organization, the Coalition Against Fur Farms also began circulating confidential research documents detailing taxpayer and fur industry supported vivisection aimed at decreasing the level of diseases and ailments that afflicted still wild animals like mink who were being forced into cages barely ten inches wide on fur farms. Other research aimed to lower financial overhead to mink farmers by developing cheaper feed sources that would not compromise the quality of the mink pelt, an economic necessity, with the recent decline of fur sales in the U.S. and Europe. Mink pelts in the early 90's were selling for as low as $22, yet farmers spent as much as $20 per animal before their pelts became marketable. A dangerously thin profit margin. Researchers and fur farmers alike identified diet as the key ingredient that led to genetic mutations that altered a wild mink's DNA to create the type of animal that fur farmers desired. Without a rigidly controlled diet, mink would return to their genetic wild origins in just two to three generations of uncontrolled breeding.

Other research focused on the side effects of this controlled breeding which in the process of creating a marketable pelt, also created a wild animal suffering from brain disorders and other physiological problems that caused animals to self mutilate themselves and cannibalize their own offspring. Other vivisectors were beginning to recognize mink as ideal models for animal research subjects because they could be housed outdoors cheaply and being predators with high metabolism, were excellent research tools for testing toxic and highly dangerous chemicals that were being dumped in the environment by industrial polluters.

While the fur industry buckled from depleted fur sales, fur farmers looked towards their research and development departments for answers that would keep them away from the edges of bankruptcy. Taxes were already levied on mink pelts at auction houses such as the Seattle Fur Exchange (SFX), earmarked specifically for fur farm research. Under the label of the Mink Farmer's Research Foundation the fur farm industry would award funds to those researchers who did the most in the field of vivisection to aid the dying fur industry.

Of all the recipients of MFRF funding, confidential records obtained by investigators revealed that year after year the number one research and development center for the fur farm industry was the Experimental Fur Animal Research Station of Oregon State University. Founded in the 1920's as a U.S. Government funded laboratory whose sole purpose was the domestication of mink and foxes for the purpose of fur production, in the 1970's the station's ownership was transferred to O.S.U. and the facility became renowned for its aid to beginning fur farmers who experienced problems common to the intensive confinement and artificial feeding of a wild native North American predator.

By the 1980's the station was seen as the nation's number one research center for experimentation on behalf of the nation's 500 plus mink farmers, having abandoned its research into fox farming due to the high cost of raising foxes in intensive confinement. The station funded itself primarily with grants from the MFRF, in addition to expensive feed donations for its research animals from the Northwest Fur Breeders Cooperative in Washington State. The station concluded its research year with the killing of its mink herd whose pelts would then be processed and marketed through the SFX as a means of raising more research revenue. This became vital when Oregon voters axed additional funding that had previously come from the unsuspecting state tax payers. Like any successful industry, research and development vitally serves the fur farm industry's needs, while on the fur farms themselves mink were being confined in conditions that commonly caused them to chew off their own tails, clip their fur and constantly scratch away at their wire enclosures in a useless attempt at freedom from their ten inch wide cages. This for an animal used to roaming up to ten miles a night and remaining solitary except during breeding and kitraising season. Most mink farms house thousands of animals divided from each other only by thin metal or plastic dividers until they are killed at seven months of age. On fox, bobcat and lynx farms animals are also housed in wire cages suspended off the ground with barely enough room to turn around. Normally sharing a cramped 3 by 4 foot square cage with their off-spring, awaiting the fur farmer who will crush them to death, anally electrocute them, gas them in a plywood box with carbon monoxide from the exhaust of a gasoline engine, shoot them or administer a lethal injection.Many fur farms are in the habitat these animals would normally live their free lives and often a mink, fox, bobcat or lynx can be seen gazing through the wire to the freedom just feet away that will never be theirs. For those of us gathered late at night huddled around a VCR watching fur farm videotapes and the photo copied pages of research papers spread around the floor, we saw something besides the physical suffering these animals go through. We saw in them what we see in ourselves, the wild spirit yearning to be free. The spirit never meant to be broken but which man's brutal science and agriculture was desperately trying to harness. We saw the fate of all of earth's creatures who as they are crowded onto the last wild places on earth, must either serve a purpose to mankinds voracious appetite of destruction and greed or disappear forever. To the fur industry, we knew that fur farming was the last stronghold of a centuries old barbaric commercial enterprise in wildlife. But in the early 1990's many in the animal rights movement were too busy spreading their focus and pursuing public acceptance to concentrate on and finish off, an industry that was slowly regaining its strength. It was time that something was done, many former ALF activists were intimidated or chose early retirement due to fears inspired by rabid FBI/ATF investigations or were too busy pursuing other forms of activism. Luckily others were unwilling to surrender to these fears and felt it was time to resurrect the Western Wildlife Unit of the ALF. The fur farm industry consisted of less than 660 farms and its research base less than ten institutions.

The killing season of 1990 would be the last that fur farmers would experience peacefully.

CHAPTER SIX
Operation Bite Back: Going for the Throat

*I*n the darkened New Moon of May 1991, we found ourselves on the roof of Oregon State University's Experimental Fur Animal Research Station. The headlights from passing cars bounced off of the five long barns containing 1,100 mink and the sounds of their scratching and the unforgettable scent of their musk was in the night air. Below, we could just make out the outlined shape of a black-clad woman whose long black hair shielded her face, a radio antenna extending from her hand. Receiving an "all-clear" a warrior lowered themself into the mink barn compound and circled the rows of cages. This was one of many reconnaissance missions whose sole purpose was to familiarize our unit the layout and night activity of the research station. The target buildings had been located and all that we lacked was an entry point. All doors were avoided as they are the obvious and most common place for alarms.

Walking amongst the mink in their cages, it wasn't long before it was discovered that a few mink were outside their cages, yet still prevented from freedom by a surrounding five foot fence topped with electric wire. As one mink approached, the warrior stood still as she sniffed their scent, then continued on in search of an opening to the nearby creek that flowed past the station. Walking to a gate in the yard and after checking it for alarms, the warrior opened it and stood back. The solitary mink approached slowly and as she crossed the threshold to freedom, bolted in a sprint to the nearby river and disappeared. Shutting the gate the warrior glanced above her to a small window and upon testing it, discovered it wasn't locked. Through the windows it became plainly obvious that this was the building that housed the archives of research records from the last 70 years of fur farm research, as well as laboratory equipment for the research performed at the station. The offices of the head researcher, Ron Scott, also adjoined the lab.

This would be one of two targets of the first raid on a fur farm research station by the Western Wildlife Unit of the ALF. The other was to be a barn containing all the experimental feed and mixing equipment that stood a safe distance and downwind from where any animals were caged. Already preliminary investigations had proven that the experimental feeds were the backbone of all research currently in progress on diets for the mink that would ensure optimum pelt quality and yet remain economically feasible. We also knew the already high cost of these feeds was being covered by the Northwest Fur Breeders Cooperative and without this donation the research station would have to cut into its research budget to provide feed for its research animals.

Drawing back from the station that night we felt elated, not sad, knowing the next visit would be the last and one the researchers would never forget. The following days were spent choosing a night for the raid that would offer adequate darkness and minimal activity on the premises and neighboring campus and houses.

In late May we received word that state charges against three accused ALF activists of a raid on University of Oregon labs in 1986 were dropped and decided what better way to celebrate this, then with another ALF raid in Oregon. As the sun lowered itself on the day of June 10, 1991 six ALF warriors found themselves gathered around a campfire on nearby forest lands checking battery power on radios, reviewing hand drawn and topographical maps, and dressing down in bright college attire to hide the dark clothes they wore underneath. A joy that rarely inhabits our ranks was in the air as we readied ourselves for a night that would bring long-awaited justice to the nation's largest fur farm research station.

Fanny packs were organized with the assorted equipment necessary to each individual member and cash was distributed to each warrior who would be on foot in case of separation, as well as maps with predetermined routes out of the area. Easy retreat plans were reviewed, roles were discussed and each warrior would repeat their responsibilities until everyone was assured that they understood every action that would comprise the raid.

With darkness among us as our greatest friend, we gathered for a last vocal moment and each expressed our reasons for being there that night and spoke of what we hoped to achieve for our mink relations. Never have I seen a finer group of warriors and as we piled into our separate vehicles, it was hard to hide my pride in this handful of people who were about to risk all for our Mother Earth. Within an hour, lookouts were in place and four warriors on mountain bikes descended into the nearby creeks that led to the station. Without a spoken word, only hand signals, we deployed ourselves to our various positions and hearing no radio warning (silence meant the all-clear) we began the nights work. While one warrior busied themselves with removing breeding identification cards from the mink cages (to confuse the researchers as there was no other way to identify the animals), two others slipped through the still unlocked bathroom window into the main records building. Research photos, slides and documents were loaded into backpacks along with the vivisector phone books, address books and other material that would reveal supporters and financiers to the stations dirty work. After this, every single file, research paper and archive in the station was spilled onto the floor and every available liquid poured onto them until a water line from the bathroom was broken that would flood the entire floor.

Following this the most expensive laboratory equipment was quietly smashed and test tube samples were dumped down the drain. Veterinary medicines that might come in handy in the future were loaded into a fanny pack and lastly, the red-spray paint came out and the WWU's calling card and suggested advice to vivisectors left behind, that and the tell tale "ALF". Exiting the research building the same way we entered, our forces began their withdrawal as the demolitions warrior and one watch person stayed behind. With a one-hour delay incendiary device the "demo" entered the experimental feed barn after the official ALF key (boltcutters) was used to obtain entry. Placing the device near the structural center of the building, the warrior then piled wooden fur farm equipment around the device, set it, and fled. Within minutes all team members regrouped carrying plastic trash bags in their fanny packs containing all tools and evidence of our presence. In a few more minutes with mountain bike loaded and all confiscated research documents and photos in a safe car, we drove the speed limit across county lines to the nearby interstate where all clothes worn during the action were distributed in various dumpsters. Shoes worn during the action also were thrown away and all tools although new were deposited in the nearest river. At about this same time a fire erupted in the experimental feed barn and demolished the feed supply and all equipment in the barn, as well as the barn itself.

Over 1,100 mink watched from their cages as the fur farm researchers arrived to survey the damage. Within minutes TV cameras were on the scene as federal and local authorities waded through 70 years of fur farm research, down the drain. Morale among the Northwest's fur farmers was at an all time low as they now wrestled with the uncomfortable fact that not only had virtually every research project at OSU's fur Animal Research Station been destroyed, but also every name and number of theirs was now in the hands of the ALF. Genetic logbooks for the research mink were also missing along with vital research records necessary for the continuation of research.

The blow was too much for the tight budgeted research lab to endure. When 1991 ended and OSU's mink herd was killed, OSU's animal research department decided to cut funds to the fur farm and within six months the Oregon State University Experimental Fur Animal Research Station closed its doors forever. In its first stage, Operation Bite Back had shutdown the nations largest Fur Farm research facility.

CHAPTER SEVEN
Biting the Hand That Feeds

*B*efore the dust could settle on the still smoldering ruins of OSU's research station, a small WWU-ALF war party was dispatched to Edmonds, Washington, home of the Northwest Fur-Breeders Cooperative. Nw Coop provided annual support to OSU's research station, not out of the goodness of its cold heart, but because its members represented the majority of fur farmers in Washington, Oregon, Idaho, and Montana, who served to benefit from OSU's research. Located on the docks of Edmonds, the NW Co-Op serves as a feed manufacturer, processing tons of factory-farm and fish by-products into the food that will keep Northwest fur farms operational. Operating as a hub, the nw Co-Op sends out diesel tractor-trailers weekly to its member fur farmers, distributing feed, nesting materials and other equipment to the fur farm industry.

On the night of June 15th, four warriors stood above the docks of Edmonds watching the 11 o'clock p.m. shift end its business for the night at the co-op from a nearby hillside. In each one of the warriors' nightpacks (to others known as daypacks) were radios with microphone and earphone extensions extending out to the raiders' shoulders much like bike cops in nearby Seattle. Once again, the trusted mountain bike war ponies were used and if anyone saw them that night, they would remember four warriors riding down from the hills above Edmonds to the docks where the four riders broke into separate directions to establish look out points at all road entry ways. One of the warriors carried a police scanner and through previous reconnaissance, had already become familiar with the "normal" radio traffic and was familiar with codes used by the police.

Two warriors went on foot, casually walking along the docks like two starstruck lovers, holding hands and stopping intermittently to survey the scene that lay before them. When they passed into the shadows behind the nw Co-Op, the two warriors quickly darted behind two tractor trailers whose refrigeration units buzzed loudly over the surrounding sounds of the docks. The smell of fish entrails permeated the air and the warriors quickly donned their dark disposable coveralls they could use to crawl through the mess. Locating an access window for feed products to enter through, they crawled into it, carefully lifting their nightpacks into the building. With continued radio silence signalling the all-clear, the two warriors quickly surveyed the empty building to ensure that no late night employees or watchman remained. Upon confirmation of an empty building, the two warriors entered the warehouse portion of the building where dry feed and nesting materials were stacked to the ceiling on wooden forklift pallets. Opening a ceiling vent to allow a little air circulation to fuel the fire, one warrior set to work assembling the incendiary device while the other left the ALF calling card accompanied with a mink paw encircled within the female symbol for the mink mothers at OSU, whose young the ALF were unable to rescue. A security patrol circled the building, but the warriors knew as long as everything appeared normal, there would be no reason for the guard to stop and investigate. Once the incendiary device was set and the patrol truck had passed, the two warriors exited quickly and quietly, stripping off their coveralls and continuing their stroll through the harbor back to their mountain bikes and the friendly dark night.

Within 90 minutes firefighters were responding to the four alarm blaze that injured no one, but effectively destroyed 75% of the nw fur breeders warehouse causing an estimated $750,000 in damages. Phase two of Operation Bite Back was complete. Following the OSU. and nw furbreeders raids the fur farm industry went ballistic. A $35,000 reward was offered for the capture and conviction of ALF warriors, and fur farmers had announced in the media that they were now arming themselves against further attacks.

The fur farm industry mouthpiece, the Fur Farm Animal Welfare Coalition held a press conference in Seattle asking animal rights groups to denounce the ALF. Granted, none publicly did at this time, but neither did one ever come forward to support the ALF except the small grassroots group Coalition Against Fur Farms who distributed press releases and attempted to organize mainstream follow-up campaigns to continue the pressure on fur farm research stations. And so the summer of '91 began with the Western Wildlife Unit back in action. Training continued, and confiscated research papers and fur farm trade journals were reviewed to determine the next link in fur farm animal abuse that could be broken. ALF moles followed up on leads of other potential targets, and searched veterinary medicine files for possible future actions.

In July, a newspaper article arrived from CAFF from Spokane, Washington describing the impact the ALF was causing on Washington State University's fur animal research. At this same time confiscated documents from OSU revealed how research programs of WSU vivisector John Gorham were groundbreaking in searching for a remedy to diseases suffered by mink on fur farms due to their intensive confinement. Within days ALF warriors were on their way to WSU, in Pullman, Washington.

CHAPTER EIGHT
The Night of Stars Falling

*A*s Animal Liberation Front moles busied themselves in researching all they could about the research of John Gorham, the foot soldiers began reconnaissance missions on the Washington State University campus that spread out across the rolling hills surrounding Pullman, Washington. Like most of southeastern Washington the Pullman area is grass covered plains devoid of trees having been mostly deforested by the timber industry. We already knew the location of the US Department of Agriculture's Experimental Fur Farm at WSU. was hidden from the public, but how difficult could it be to find unmistakable mink barns?

Our first step was the now tried and true tactic of riding mountain bikes like casual bicyclists on every road, trail and path that crisscrossed the WSU campus. Checking outlying buildings and keeping our noses to the wind for the easily recognizable scent of mink musk. Meanwhile, the moles had discovered that WSU is a nerve center of animal research on native American wildlife. Grizzly and black bears, mule deer, elk and bighorn sheep were just a few of the animals we soon discovered wallowing in the misery of concrete pens and corrals. Serving as a prostitute to the livestock industry, WSU vivisectors were busying themselves in studying bacterial and competitive grazing threats native wildlife posed to cattle and sheep grazed on public lands. Never before had the ALF discovered vivisection on America's wildlife outside of OSU's mink farm and now our strategist and logistics experts were discussing ways to transport these larger animals. Unfortunately, our resources and warrior shortages would prohibit us spiriting away bears or deer this time... Our focus remained the mink. The newspaper article we had received had also discussed a furbearer research facility also on campus, where vivisector Fred Gilbert tested underwater traps on beavers. His lab also housed wolverine, fishers, badgers, and martens. We would also attempt to locate Gilbert's laboratory and liberate the wildlife prisoners there. Gilbert's research was funded by the Canadian fur industry. John Gorham's research was not only funded by the Mink Farmers Research Foundation, but also by the US Department of Agriculture. Gorham targeted Aluetian Disease, Encephalopathy (known in cattle as Mad Cow Disease) and other diseases that could economically wipe out a fur farmer should mink become affected. To conduct his research, Gorham would grind up infected mink brains and force-feed them to healthy mink until they contracted the chosen disease. Animals in his laboratory often died slow deaths as the paralysis of their disease slowly developed in their bodies, causing nervous disorders and hemorrhaging. Fur farmers across the world had identified John Gorham as "one of the worlds leading researchers in fur farm diseases", according to an article in Fur Rancher Magazine, in 1991.

After locating the fur farm on WSU.'s campus, hidden in plain sight off a road to the local airport, a nighttime recon was planned. In the early evening of a full moon before the lunar rising, two warriors hiked to the fur farm where they scaled a chain-link fence topped with barbed-wire to reach the mink barns. The perimeter was walked until it was determined that no infra-red or motion detector alarms surrounded the facility. Being a federally funded research station, we expected as much. There wasn't any electronic security.

The warriors surveyed the area and quickly located the control group mink who had not been infected with any disease. Once the layout of the facility became familiar and no premise watchmen or watchdogs were located, the warriors pulled back to the chain-link fence. From a distance a car could be heard approaching so the two warriors quickly climbed the fence when one warrior was snagged by barbed-wire. As the headlights, of the oncoming car became visible, the trapped warrior wrestled with their pant leg, finally freeing themselves and jumping from the fence and sprinting across the road to cover just as the car approached and passed. It was a police car. As the two warriors walked in the pre-moon darkness, they noticed the headlight beams of the police car had made a 360 turn and then went out. As the two warriors walked the shoulder of the road they became suspicious. Pulling out a pair of binoculars the warriors sighted in the distance the outline of a car parked on the shoulder of the road with its lights off, on a crash course with the warriors. Quickly the two darted into the surrounding bare hillside, jUSt as another police cruiser came speeding from the opposite direction on the same road. The first police cruiser gunned its engine and turned on its headlights in an attempt to sandwich in the two warriors. As the warriors scrambled into the kneehigh grass the two police cars came together at the fur farm and began to shine spotlights into the facility, then the surrounding hillsides. This fur farm research facility was obviously expecting a visit from the ALF.

As the two warriors lay on their bellies in the sparse hills surrounding the fur farm, the moon rose clear and bright, illuminating the whole area. One police cruiser inched with its lights off just feet past the two hiding warriors and parked on a ridge overlooking the entire fur farm compound. As the warriors remained motionless, coyotes began to howl as the moon lifted itself into the sky. Something sounded out of place, as most of the coyote cries were concentrated, and coming from the direction of a small building above the fur farm. Still other coyotes could be heard howling from the distant hills. It became plainly evident that in one of the buildings above the fur farm coyotes were held captive. With little to do but wait it out, the two warriors cursed themselves for being trapped under the moon's bright light. Finally the police cruiser gave up the hunt and drove away and the warriors hiked the long way back to their hidden mountain bikes. The element for a surprise attack was gone. Not only had Washington State University's animal researchers had the OSU and NW furbreeders raid as a warning, but now university police had spotted trespassers near the hidden fur farm. Within days, security was increased and when Fred Gilbert's lab was finally located nestled in a grove of pine trees, an infra-red perimeter security system was seen in place. The beaver sheds were clearly visible just beyond it.

Despite the increased security, cautious reconnaissance continued and soon a kennel was located on a hill containing 12 coyotes, the subjects of sarcocystis research. Sarcocystis is a disease that is not fatal to coyotes or sheep, the disease passes through a coyote's system in a few short weeks, while the parasites contain themselves within sheep, destroying the economic value of their meat and wool. Coyotes commonly spread the parasite in their feces where it is transmitted to sheep who are grazed on public lands in coyote country. The coyotes for these experiments were conveniently provided by the US Department of Agriculture's Animal Damage Control Program. Survivors of aerial gunning and gassed out dens where their families perished.

A strategy session was called to discuss the future of any actions at WSU.'s fur research stations and it was decided that in order for any successful attack, warriors with various degrees of experience would be needed. By mid-August, seven ALF warriors confirmed their willingness to risk an attack on the already on-guard fur animal research departments of WSU. Moles informed the Operation Bite Back team that John Gorham had been chosen as the USDA's "Researcher of the Year" for 1991, and would be out of town the week of August 21st to receive his award. It was time to act. The raid would be a three-pronged attack. One team would enter the Veterinary Building on WSU.'s downtown Pullman campus where Gorham's office was located, another would strike the fur farm and a third would release the coyotes from their hill top kennel.

In a motel room miles from Pullman, ALF warriors gathered around maps while others scanned local police frequencies. Except for the designated drivers, the remaining warriors divided heavy gloves to the mink handlers, forced entry tools to the Veterinary Building team and boltcutters and red spraypaint to the coyote liberators. A medium of communication was agreed upon for necessary radio transmissions and pick up-points and times were finalized. Already all the team members had been driven through the area pointing out spots near the road where warriors would be dropped off and animals picked up. This time there would be no full moon, but there would be meteor showers according to weather forecasters. When the final emergency contingency plan was understood should the police become aware of our raid, the warriors drove away in the direction to Washington State University.

The first team arrived at the Veterinary Building just as a late night student exited the bottom level. One warrior moved to a lookout position while another located a door latch that had earlier been tampered with so that all that was needed was an aggressive pull to detach the lockplate that held the pin of the door lock. Climbing the stairwell to the 3rd floor level where Gorham's office was located, ALF warriors entered the lit hallway and removed a ceiling tile in the hallway outside Gorham's office. In the ceiling crawl space only thin sheetrock separated the hallway from Gorham's office on the other side of the wall partition. With a small key-hole saw, a hole was punched through and ALF warriors were in "one of the world's leading fur farm researchers" office.

Computer discs, photo slides and address books were removed and a brand new computer for Johnny Boy lay still in the box beside his desk. Lifting the computer over her head a warrior smashed it to the ground and proceeded to do the same to every piece of research and computer equipment in the room, the ALF version of therapy. Meanwhile another warrior dumped every file of Gorham's on the floor until the pile was over a foot thick across the office. As a final touch two gallons of muriatic acid was poured over the complete mess until fumes forced the warriors out of the office. As the warriors exited down the hallway, they passed a gurney with a plexiglass box filled with white mice with a label reading "irradiated 8/21/91" grabbing the box under one arm the warriors fled the building, completing phase one of the attack on WSU. At about the same time as the Veterinary Building was being entered, four ALF warriors were dropped off out of sight of the mink barns and coyote kennels. Splitting into two groups, one approached the mink barns, the other the coyote kennels. At the mink barns a watchman was now living on the premises, but would go to sleep after an 11 p.m. check on the mink barns. Approaching the watchman's window, an ALF warrior peered in to hear the sweet sound of loud snoring. Returning to the mink barns, the official ALF key was used to cut the small padlock on the barn door and two warriors entered the control animal barn with a wire cage with six separate compartments. One by one mink were coaxed into the cage until it was full.

Leaving the barn one raider replaced the cut lock with a similar duplicate in case the watchman decided to conduct a visual inspection later that night he would see nothing out of place. Each warrior carrying one handle of the mink cage, the two figures disappeared into the darkness. Back on the hilltop coyote kennel, one warrior busied themselves clearing low fencing surrounding the kennel with boltcutters to provide an escape from the area for the coyotes, while the other cut the lock leading to the kennel and entered. Moving down the cages the coyotes became anxious as they anticipated this late night visit as a friendly one. The coyotes had been visited regularly by the ALF so were accustomed to the strangers with covered faces. One by one, cage doors were opened and coyotes leapt out towards the door of the kennel.

While most of the coyotes fled the area immediately, others could be heard in the distance, howling from the dark shadows of the wild as we had heard them before. Meanwhile, one coyote hung back attempting to sneak past the liberator to the last cage. The warrior then noticed the last caged coyote to be a young female who eyed the hesitant coyote with anticipation. As the liberator swung open the last cage, the two coyotes bolted off together into the darkness as stars shot across the sky in a magical brilliance. Tears soaked the liberator's face mask as they realized the love these last two coyotes had for one another, so strong that one refused to leave this hell until the other was also free. As coyote shapes disappeared across the plains, the masked coyote warriors took a spraypaint can and painted in large letters across the back of the now empty coyote kennel: "American wildlife, love it or leave it alone – freedom for fur animals now!!!"

As the sun rose the following day, the evidence of the raid was quickly discovered by veterinary students who normally fed the now-free coyotes. As the authorities were alerted both vivisectors and WSU. Administrators were furious that they had had the wool pulled over their eyes by the cagey ALF. Fur animal researchers attempted to deny that research projects were funded by the fur industry, only to be dispelled by ALF released documents stating the contrary. Though Fred Gilbert's laboratory escaped the attack, his experiments did not. A Seattle TV station had filed a legal action against Gilbert and Washington State University for the release of his videotaped underwater trap experiments on beavers. Citing that the videotapes were the property of the funder, the Fur Institute of Canada,

Gilbert refused to release the tapes, while Washington residents were shocked that their university was being used to benefit the Canadian fur industry. Within a year Fred Gilbert quit his post as the head of the Fur Bearer Research Facility and retreated to a British Columbia University to continue his work, out of the US For Gorham, his selection as Researcher of the Year was tarnished by the destruction of his on-going research which was rendered useless by stolen computer records and acid-damaged files, slides and records. Gorham attempted to distance himself from fur farm research only to later be featured on the cover of Fur Rancher Magazine in late 1991 as an honored guest on tour of Russian fur farms overseas.

While the fur farm industry mourned the loss of the second largest recipient of Mink Farmer Research Foundation funded research, six mink began their new lives on the banks of the Lochsa River on the nearby Nez Perce Reservation. As summer turned to fall, a coyote family began its preparations for the coming winter, their tattooed ears covered over by thickening fur, never would they forget the Night of Stars Falling and their human relations who freed them.

CHAPTER NINE
Down on the Farm

*B*y September of 1991 US fur farm and Federal law enforcement forces began to anticipate an all out war by the ALF. Photographs of known fur farm activists were being circulated among fur farmers and caution was being exercised when hiring farm help. The '91 pelting season was drawing near and with it the anxiety among fur farmers that they would be the next target of the ALF. Fears were justified, when in the end of September an unsuccessful attempt was made to burn down the Utah Fur Breeders Cooperative in Sandy, Utah where feeds for the state with the largest amount of fur farms were produced. The rural cooperative also housed a mink farm on its premises which was also used for experimentation in fur farm research.

Not to be discouraged, the ALF activists returned to the northwest where once again vigilant security forces almost discovered ALF raiders on their farms and the fur farmers were poised to attack. The war party then traveled to a mink farm outside of Olympia, Washington where a four-person party was deployed on the perimeter of the mink farms guard fence surrounding the mink barns. While others stood watch, one warrior began surveying the farm searching out the breeder mink, the most valuable part of the herd. Crouched in the darkness the warrior watched as another human form approached casually with a flashlight in hand. Thinking the approaching human to be one of the other members of the war party, the lone warrior remained crouched in the open while the human form approached. When the figure retreated before seeing the warrior, the ALF warrior returned to the waiting party.

"Whats up?", "Nothing, why?" "Wasn't that you that just came near me?" "We've been right here." There was a watchman patrolling the barns. In a slow retreat the raiders were forced to abandon their attack, once again escaping confrontation with fur farmers.

At this time, an ALF mole alerted the Operation Bite Back team to a fur farm up for sale near Salem, Oregon just down the road from OSU The fur farmer, Hynek Malecky, was interested in not just selling his mink operation, but maintaining a partnership in a joint venture. Benefiting directly from OSU's research, Malecky had developed a state-of-the-art mink operation and now with the declining market in mink pelts, he needed additional financing to keep his business alive. No bank would dare loan a fur farmer money not only because of the instability of the fur market, but also because of the recent attacks by the ALF. Malecky Mink Farm was only one of many fur farms teetering on the edge of bankruptcy. The Western Wildlife Unit of the ALF decided to give it a little push.

In early December, long cold rainy nights of reconnaissance had revealed almost no security on the mink farm surrounded by adjoining ranches. What was difficult was approaching the fur farm through the patchwork of private residences that surrounded it. It was decided that a three-person team would be adequate on this action. One driver and two mountain bike riding warriors launched the attack. On December 10th on a still evening the ALF driver dropped off two warriors and their trusty steeds on the narrow country road leading towards Malecky Mink Farm. Donning dark blue raingear and hooded sweaters the two warriors swooped towards their target, their small nightpacks on their backs carrying the tools necessary to carry out the action.

One warrior monitored an open radio channel with the ALF driver who sat in their truck a few miles away monitoring the police scanner. The local Radio Shack had provided radio frequencies for law enforcement in the area as they normally do for scanner-buffs. The "demo" warrior remained radio-less so that she could keep her senses attuned to every sound around her, with her long black hair braided behind her neck to prevent loose hairs from not only snagging on fences, but also to insure no DNA traceable clues would be left behind. With the radio-warrior in place within sight of both the Malecky home and the target building and the advancing demo warrior, the two exchanged a thumbs-up in the darkness and the demo warrior disappeared into the pelt processing and feed mixing building which served as the heart of the operation. Separate from the mink barns, the nerve center of the operation housed feed mixing equipment, refrigeration units, drying drums for the mink pelts, skinning racks and the assorted supplies necessary to keep a mink farm operational. Standing in the darkened processing building the warrior imagined the farm in full operation, the mobile gas chambers unloading still quivering mink to the waiting skinners, the smells of musk while the pelts are stripped from the minks warm bodies like banana peels. Returning to the present the warrior was glad that would be a scene never experienced again at Malecky Mink Ranch. First locating the structural center of the building, the warrior then identified it to be of wooden framework. Gathering mink nesting boxes, pelt-stretching boards and other flammable available materials, the warrior built a pyramid of combustible materials and then placed the one-hour kitchen-timer delayed incendiary device beneath the whole mess. Setting a series of flammable liquids in open plastic containers surrounding the device the warrior twisted the dial on the timer, connected the nine-volt battery and slowly fled the building mentally noting on her watch when the device should trigger. By the time the warriors rendezvoused with their pick-up driver, there were still 36 minutes left before the device ignited. Thirty-two minutes later the device ignited and before fire trucks could reach the scene the heart of Malecky Mink Farm lay in ruins. One fur farm down, 600 to go. The action was clean and smooth and by the time Federal investigators arrived on the scene, the only evidence they found was a burned down fur farm. Not even the telltale "ALF" was spray painted anywhere. The warriors had decided that to do so would only leave evidence that might narrow the scope of suspects. Spray painting would only help law enforcement to conclude that the fire was arson and not accidental or an insurance scam. This action which took place after the pelting season insured that there was not only a minimal risk of harming animals on the farm since most had already been killed, but also cost the fur farmer expensive pelts which were still in the processing building.

Chapter Ten
The Michigan Mink Militia

$\mathcal{B}$efore 1991 came to an end an attempt was made to destroy the pelt processing operation of Huggan's Rocky Mountain Fur Company outside of Hamilton, Montana. The fur company, which also operated its own mink and fox farm, processes pelts for most mink farms in Western Montana. Montana is also home to many of the US's lynx and bobcat farms, with Fraser Fur Farm in Ronan, Montana boasting the largest wildcat fur farm in the country. As the 1991 pelting season came to a close, after being on the alert since the June ALF attacks, many fur farmers breathed a sigh of relief hoping the brunt of Operation Bite Back was over. Nothing could be further from the truth. In January of 1992, People for the Ethical Treatment of Animals ran a series of radio announcements in western Michigan drawing attention to Michigan State University's animal experiments by Richard Aulerich whose primary laboratory animal "models" were mink. Unbeknownst to PETA, Richard Aulerich was also the second largest recipient of annual grants by the Mink Farmers Research Foundation and had for the past 32 years provided vital research developments to the US mink industry. Any discussion of mink farm disease research never omitted Aulerich from the conversation. ALF moles repeatedly found his research developments cited in correspondence seized from OSU and WSU.

Through his service to the US Government and the mink industry, Aulerich had been awarded federal grants to also use his mink farm for toxic experiments involving the force-feeding of pcp's, dioxins and other industrial pollutants to captive mink. Published research records detailed how poisoned mink died violent deaths in Aulerich's laboratory suffering severe internal hemorrhaging before vomiting blood and finally dying after being fed only feeds laced with contaminants, in the infamous Lethal Dose 50% (ld50) test.

Students at MSU had informed ALF moles that a 39-mile stretch of the lower Fox River which feeds Lake Michigan, is home to the largest concentration of paper mills in the world. Despite pcp productions having been banned almost 20 years ago, these pollutants still remain from early discharges in the mud and sediment along the river and lake causing high levels of pcp in fish and other wildlife. Another area situated at the mouth of the Grand Calumet River at the southern end of Lake Michigan, has the largest accumulation of industry contaminated sediments in the Great Lakes. Students were frustrated that despite all dioxin in the Great Lakes being traced to less than 200 factory stacks and all pcp traceable to five industries, the only remedies were to entrust these corporations to voluntarily clean up, or continue animal testing of the contaminants to determine its danger. A 1990 "study" showed 100% mortality among test animals exposed to sediment samples from the Grand Calumet River.

Rather than study contamination in wild mink and otters in the Great Lakes region, Aulerich chose to cause further suffering by using mink and otters from his fur farm in experiments. ALF moles had also been given information by students about Aulerich making keychains for his students out of the severed paws of vivisected mink. One of Aulerich's research associates was Karen Chou who herself conducted toxicology experiments in rabbits, rats and mice for chemical manufacturers, industrial polluters and the US Government. To the American mink industry, Richard Aulerich represented the last hope for the conquering of diseases commonly found on fur farms. OSU's Experimental Research Station was out of the game, and John Gorham's research was in tatters. The Fur Animal Research Station at Michigan State University was on alert against attacks by the ALF following the raids in Oregon and Washington. When peta radio spots fingered Aulerich, MSU increased its already strengthened security. In the midst of fur farmer and research hysteria, a council of ALF warriors was formed on behalf of the Lake Michigan Ecosystem to stop the suffering to mink at the hands of Aulerich and to draw attention to the real threat: industrial polluters.

As a light rain fell in the February night on the mink barns at MSU three figures lay crouched low to the earth in woodland camouflage. As cars rumbled by on a nearby highway, the warriors cut through chain link fences and entered the perimeter of the Experimental Fur Farm. At this same time another ALF cell from the newly formed Great Lakes Unit was walking towards Anthony Hall on the Michigan State University campus like three college students returning home from a late night drinking session. One of the warriors had an earphone beneath his hooded sweatshirt that kept the team in contact with a lookout parked in a car nearby monitoring a police scanner. With no signal, the three activists cut across the lawn in front of the building and dropped into a storm drain depression below a bottom story window. The latch on the window was ajar and with a long thin strip of metal a warrior slid the latch open and opened the window and two warriors slipped into the building landing on the desk of an MSU researcher. Closing the window behind them, the third warrior removed his bright college sweater and replaced it with a black hooded rain jacket and kept watch.

Inside the building the other two warriors walked the lit hallway to a stairway and up one level to the office of Richard Aulerich. During early daytime reconnaissance in the building, the warriors had viewed the open office door, not noticing any type of entry way alarm system in place. While one warrior stood watch against late night students in the building, the other broke through three wooden vent slats on the door and reached through and opened the door and ducked in. Aulerich and Chou's office lay before them with a receptionist area, complete with a glass case filled with mink pelts for display. Opening all the file drawers in every office and dumping their contents on the floor, the warrior removed his pack and opened a tupperware container that contained a one-hour time delay incendiary device cushioned with toilet paper.

Suddenly, flashing red and blue lights could be seen through the windows. The warrior knew if it was cause for alarm, he would have been alerted by one of their two lookouts. Continuing in his task, the warrior filled his nightpack with computer discs, color slides and selected research documents describing grants for continued vivisection. In a few short minutes the patrol car drove away as did the motorist he had pulled over, and the warrior set the incendiary device and gathering his lookout, returned to the basement level office.

Before the warriors exited the window they glanced at the office of the researcher they had entered in through. The nameplate outside the door had said "dairy research". The warriors, both Vegans, looked at each other then slid all the computers and office equipment on his desk onto the floor with a crash. Then the two rolled out the window into the storm drain and with a quick clothing adjustment returned on their path walking off campus. The pick-up driver pulled up to them a short distance away and in minutes they were safely off campus.

Back at the fur farm neighboring the poultry research farm, one warrior stationed himself with a clear view of all incoming roads and the occupied quarters of the sleeping caretaker. One warrior ascended the roof of the field laboratory and removed a portion of sheet metal roofing and dropped into the lab through the ceiling. Without any exposed windows to the outdoors, two warriors switched on headlamps tinted red to preserve their night vision and began to remove hinges on a door leading into a laboratory. Upon entering, one warrior began to quietly destroy all the research equipment, while the other searched files and research records. Muriatic acid was poured over feed mixing machinery for the experimental mink farm as well as over all the research equipment and documents that were in the offices. In a freezer the warriors found the severed heads of over 30 otters wrapped in aluminum foil. When the laboratory feed mixing room and a research office were wrecked, spraypainted messages were left for Aulerich and other researchers, including "we will be back for the otters", meaning Alice, the sole surviving experimental otter prisoner who watched attentively as ALF warriors raided the fur farm. Exiting the lab through the ceiling, the two warriors entered the perimeter of the mink farm itself and began to remove every identification card from the mink cages, first locating two minks slated for contamination, yet still healthy. Borrowing two nestboxes the mink were loaded into the boxes separately for their journey to freedom. The close busy highway prohibited the liberators from opening all the cages and releasing all the mink. Night began to give way to dawn's early light. The hardest part was leaving behind the hundreds of other minkas well as ferrets and otters that we knew would soon be poisoned.

Hours later on the shores of a remote lake the two liberated mink were given their last meal by human hands, a road-killed rabbit and protein rich wet catfood before being released into their native habitat where they quickly disappeared into the lakes underbrush. Back on the MSU campus, within the hour, a fire erupted in Anthony Hall that totally destroyed 32 years of fur animal research by Richard Aulerich and over ten years of unpublished research by Karen Chou. With this final attack, all major recipients of Mink Farmer Research Foundation funding were effectively neutralized leaving the u.s. fur farm industry struggling more than ever to survive. Never before had the alf successfully eliminated the research and development arm of an animal and earth abuse industry as it did with the mfrf. As the alf earned its title, of an effective threat to animal and earth abuse industry research, warriors from across the nation began to feel the oncoming wave of federal police repression as joint law enforcement task forces accelerated their hunt for the ALF renegades.

CHAPTER ELEVEN
Until the Last Fur Farm Burns to the Ground...

In September of 1995 fur farmers and federal agents rejoiced over the beginning of a long prison sentence for admitted ALF warrior Rod Coronado. Boasting that the ALF's back had been broken, FBI and ATF agents boasted on how since Coronado's arrest little or no ALF action had been reported against the fur farm industry.

Federal investigators had moved into Syracuse, New York to uproot a growing ALF cell there and met with little success against the local network of young committed activists. The ATF had sent a message via Coronado's lawyers in Michigan that the successful tactics of the new Coalition Against the Fur Trade in Memphis, Tennessee had drawn their attention. CAFT's no compromise stance against the fur trade and its unequivocal support for the ALF made it the same type of threat that Coronado's Coalition Against Fur Farms had been in the early 1990's.

Contrary to what the FBI would want the public to believe, the ALF was anything but dead. Like a Phoenix rising from the ashes, the ALF struck four fur farms in the 1995 winter pelting season releasing mink and fox from their cages. In Chilliwack, British Columbia in October 2,400 mink were released from the Dargatz mink farm into the surrounding forest in the first major mink liberation in North America claimed by the ALF. Less than a month later the ALF struck again, this time releasing 4,000 mink from the Rippin Fur Farm in Aldergrove, British Columbia despite a security patrol hired after the first raid. Not to be outdone by their Canadian counterparts American ALF warriors struck outside Olympia, Washington, releasing 200 mink from Clarence Jordan's mink farm the same week, the same farm warriors had been chased away from back in 1991. Also 30 foxes from a Tennessee fur farm were released from their cages in late 1995.

Shortly after the raids, the Canada Mink Breeders Association posted a $50,000 reward for information leading to the conviction of ALF activists. Many of the released mink were recovered but still hundreds escaped. The economic damage to mink farms is not only measured by the actual loss of mink but also due to the confusion caused when a fur farms breeding stock is mixed amongst mink raised for pelting. Once a mink is out of its cage, it's nearly impossible to distinguish it from any other. In this way, years of selective breeding is lost and the fur farmer must begin again to isolate breeding mink based on pelt characteristics and fur quality. The raids also struck only days before the pelting season, a time that often makes or breaks a fur farm. Fur farmers claimed that farm raised mink stood a minimal chance of survival in the wild yet virtually the whole present mink populations of Iceland and England are made up of mink farm escapees. Also in Newfoundland, Scandinavia and the former Soviet Union, viable wild populations of mink have begun with unintentional releases from fur farms. In the truest act of animal liberation and wildlife preservation North American activists can strike a blow against the fur industry while at the same time helping to reintroduce a depleted native predator back into its natural habitat.

1996 began with another ALF raid on the Wisconsin fur farm of Bob Zimbal outside of Sheboygan, this time releasing 200 mink from the breeding population. Following the January raid in the leading state for mink pelt production, the Fur Commission USA increased the reward to $70,000 for information leading to the conviction of any ALF warriors in either Canada or the U.S.

Clearly it could be seen what the fur industry feared most, not protests, not negative media coverage, but illegal direct actions. The only form of activism for which the corporations and courtrooms cannot control. Not to be intimidated by the rekindled international investigation of the ALF, nor the $70,000 reward, ALF warriors struck another mink farm, this time the L.W. Bennet and Sons fur farm in Ontario County, New York in April 1996, releasing 3,000 mink from their cages of which more than a thousand escaped recapture. Since the raid, the fur farmers have stated that the ALF has pushed them closer to the edge of bankruptcy and lay-offs of farm employees will be necessary. The Canadian and American fur industry has raised rewards for the capture of the ALF to $100,000. More than five times the amount offered for the capture of violent criminals guilty of rape, murder or child abuse. And the battle continues. In June, 1996, on the fifth anniversary of the launching of Operation Bite Back, ALF warriors returned to the Utah Fur Breeders Cooperative liberating 75 mink being subjected to nutritional research at the Sandy, Utah facility.

As the 1990's continue, the ALF is showing no signs of weakness as more and more activists become disenchanted with less effective legitimate means of reform in their attempt to lay a barbaric industry to rest. Four hundred years of death and destruction is enough.

There are currently less than 500 fur farms left in the United States and now more than ever, ALF inspired direct action is quite possible the most effective tactic of putting them out of business. What remains to be seen is whether the grassroots radical environmental and animal liberation movements will be brave enough to stand up to the police repression that comes to movements that have proven to be a sincere threat to business interests destroying our planet and its last native wildlife. Clearly, the message from the ALF is as it appeared in the press release from the Oregon State University Experimental Fur Farm raid five years ago: "Until the last fur farm burns to the ground... expect to hear from us".

CHAPTER TWELVE
The Hunt for A.L.F. Warriors

*I*t was a bright and cool spring morning in the Little Applegate River Valley of Southern Oregon in April '92 when they arrived. Flying below the ridgeline the helicopter came into view just as four sedans with government plates curved the graveled dirt road. As the helicopter landed in a clearing, four ATF agents exited and ran towards the door of a nearby cabin surprising its lone occupant, a woman in her late 40s. In the cars were more ATF agents who secured the road. Demanding answers the ATF agents searched the woman's house and investigated the premises. When the agents told the startled woman they were looking for Rod Coronado she interceded and told them they had the wrong cabin, Coronado lived across the river in a separate cabin hidden in the trees. Rushing to the far side of the river the agents found the cabin which was completely empty, a single hawk feather left dangling from the doorway.

Just 15 miles from Ashland, the former headquarters of the Coalition Against Fur Farms (CAFF) was the first target of FBI and ATF harassment. Following the raid at WSU, CAFF, spokesperson Rod Coronado began to speak out against the horrors of fur farming after having completed an 11 month undercover investigation that culminated in the rescue, rehabilitation and release of 60 mink, four bobcats and two Canadian lynx from a Montana fur farm. Unfortunately for Coronado and fortunately for the police, Coronado was the only activist to go on camera in support of Operation Bite Back.

Already Coronado's parents had been harassed since fall 1991, being asked questions about Coronado's whereabouts and whether he was organizing illegal activities from his parents home. Meanwhile FBI agents had served a search warrant on the residence of a former PETA employee in Maryland, carting away boxes of papers, maps, electronic equipment and other evidence the FBI claimed detailed ALF planned raids and press materials.

A week before the search warrant was executed, a Federal Express employee pulled a package that was labeled with an expired account number and upon investigation discovered the senders address was fake.

The package was addressed to the former PETA employee. Inside the package was a videotape documenting the liberation of two mink from MSU.'s experimental fur farm and footage of the severed otter heads found in the laboratory. The package also contained stolen records, slides and computer discs from Richard Aulerich's office. When the FBI raided the receiver's house, they claimed to have discovered one of the ALF's safe houses and found infra-red night-vision goggles and aborted plans to liberate the remaining *Silver Springs Monkeys* who PETA had fought to win the legal release of for over ten years.

In the FBI's search warrant there was described a list of incendiary device materials that had been found at OSU. and MSU. The FBI also claimed that Coronado was responsible for the ALF attack on WSU in the search warrant.

Back in September of '91 a composite sketch of two suspected ALF members began to circulate after the two were seen in and near Pullman, Washington before the ALF raid. Attached to the composite sketches was a $35,000 reward for the capture and conviction the those responsible for the OSU, NW Furbreeders and WSU raids. Federal Grand Juries in Oregon, Washington and Michigan had convened to gather evidence to hopefully issue indictments against ALF members. PETA employees who had handled press materials related to the MSU. raid were subpoenaed as were PETA employee records and photos. The investigative reporter who had interviewed Coronado about Operation Bite Back was also subpoenaed. When Coronado heard the FBI wanted to question him he decided it was time to take a break from his anti-fur farm work, not wanting to engage in a lengthy and costly legal battle. At about this same time in late Spring '92 other volunteers from CAFF began being harassed by FBI and ATF agents. Next a storage unit belonging to Coronado in Ashland was raided by the ATF where agents claimed to find evidence connecting Coronado to the ALF raids in Oregon, and Washington and attempts in Montana.

Using Coronado's own writings in support of Operation Bite Back as well as threads of physical evidence, a case began to be built around Coronado while the inter-agency task force assigned to squash the ALF continued its search for other ALF members. FBI records on Coronado had him involved with illegal direct action since 1986 when he and another man sank two Icelandic whaling ships and demolished a whale processing plant. Since then Coronado had also been arrested in Canada for destruction of fur shop property. Jumping bail, Coronado fled the country in 1987 and returned to the US where the ALF was most active, in California.

Other activists from the California animal rights scene were soon subpoenaed, one of them being Jonathan Paul, a known associate of Coronado's and also one of three men who were indicted in Oregon in

1990 on charges relating to the ALF raid on the University of Oregon in 1986. Jonathan Paul was also suspect in numerous ALF actions in California as well as the toppling of powerlines on Earth Day 1990.

Paul also was a partner in the fur farm investigation that helped lead to Operation Bite Back. Exerting pressure on Paul to testify at the Washington State Grand Jury, the US Government hoped to gather information that would lead to the indictment of other suspected ALF warriors. When Paul pled the Fifth Amendment and refused to testify, he was granted immunity from prosecution and when he still refused to testify he was imprisoned on contempt of court charges, the Judge believing that imprisonment would coerce Paul to testify. He was wrong. Paul sat in jail tight lipped for six months before his imprisonment was deemed to be punishment rather than coercion and he was released. By the time Paul was released, the FBI had already shifted its focus onto Rik Scarce, the author of the book "Eco-Warriors" which contained interviews with both Coronado and ALF members. Scarce was also a student teacher at WSU and had befriended Coronado who sometimes visited his Pullman home. Scarce's fiance was also subpoenaed to the Grand Jury where she answered questions about Coronado and other CAFF volunteers.

Shortly after the ATF raid on CAFF's Oregon cabin headquarters, US Custom agents, FBI and ATF agents again attempted to capture Coronado. In the Santa Cruz harbor in California, the marine-mammal protection ship Sea Shepherd was preparing to depart on a campaign against Japanese driftnet fishing when it was ordered to stop engines by US Customs in a heavy rainstorm. ATF, FBI and US Customs agents searched the vessel to no avail. The ship would be searched again in British Columbia by Canadian authorities assisting US authorities in their own search for ALF fugitives. Coronado, a frequent volunteer with Sea Shepherd, had been seen on the Sea Shepherd before it left Los Angeles on its way to Santa Cruz.

Later the office manager of Sea Shepherd's Marina Del Rey office would be repeatedly harassed and subpoenaed because of her suspected connections with Coronado. She had purchased his car from him while still in LA Acting on information seized in the Maryland house of the former PETA employee, in the summer of '92 a Grand Jury was convened in Louisiana to investigate the leads on the aborted plans to raid the Delta Regional Primate Facility of Tulane University. By the end of 1992 over 30 activists had been subpoenaed, many of them testifying about their knowledge of the ALF.

Friends of Animals in Connecticut who had financed CAFF's undercover investigation of US fur farming cooperated fully with the authorities. 1992 would be remembered as the year that intimidated dozens of grassroots activists as more and more people in the animal rights and radical environmental movement saw firsthand the repression the FBI and ATF was causing to those activists who supported ALF and Earth First! direct action warriors. Despite this intimidation, a handful of activists weathered the storm and refused to be intimidated by the Jackbooted Nazis' of the US Government. In Spring of '93 two CAFF volunteers became the target of federal harassment. Deborah Stout and Kimberly Trimiew would soon follow the path of Jonathan Paul to jail. Already Rik Scarce was currently in the county jail in Spokane, Washington for refusing to testify about his relationship with the ALF and Coronado.

Not only activists themselves were dealt Federal subpoenas to the Grand Juries, soon activists parents were also called before the inquisitors. Meanwhile, state governments and Congress were fighting for the passage of legislation specifically tailored to target ALF and Earth First! saboteurs. It wasn't long until every state visited by the ALF passed "animal industries protection acts" that boosted any ALF-type raid to an instant felony punishable with huge fines and up to ten years in prison.

In July of 1993 a federal indictment was issued out of the Western District of Michigan naming Rod Coronado as the sole defendant, charged with the arson and break-in at MSU. Within days Coronado's face was placed on the "Most Wanted" list of the FBI, ATF and US Marshals. Though Congress and law enforcement knew the ALF to be a large well-structured organization the authorities could only build a case against Coronado due to his history and association with illegal direct action.

Attempting to use a little fish to catch a big one, the US Government had made a strategic decision to place all the blame on Coronado until evidence surfaced that would lead to indictments of other ALF warriors. Once again the forces of destruction that plagued our mother earth and her animal children had placed a price on the head of an indigenous warrior who fought to defend native American wildlife and wilderness.

CHAPTER THIRTEEN
The Last Bite: Animal Damaged Control

$\mathcal{M}$ost people would think with four grand juries and a multidivisional task force of FBI, ATF, state, university and county police forces investigating the ALF, that the warriors were hunkered in hiding from the law. The ALF was hiding, but not only from the law. The sun was setting on a warm autumn day as three figures passed binoculars back and forth, gazing from a ridge on national forest lands in Utah at the US Department of Agriculture's Animal Damage Control Predator Research Facility located in Millville, just south of the University of Utah campus in Logan; the ADC field station is the largest research station in the US that performs vivisection on coyotes, the objective being not saving lives, but destroying them.

For 65 years ADC has waged with full taxpayer support, a war on America's wildlife. In 1931 Congress passed the Animal Damage Control Act which plainly states: "The Secretary of Agriculture is hereby authorized to promulgate the best methods of eradication, suppression, or bringing under control on … areas of public domain or private lands, of wolves, lions, coyotes, bobcats, prairie dogs, … injurious to agriculture and animal husbandry, for the protection of stock and other domestic animals … and to conduct campaigns for the destruction of control of such animals." Since its beginnings, ADC has been responsible for the murder of hundreds of thousands of grizzly and black bears, grey, red, swift and kit foxes, grey and timber wolves, mountain lions, bobcats, lynx, jaguars, mink, moose, elk, pronghorn antelope, bighorn sheep, blacktail, whitetail and mule deer, buffalo and coyotes.

Their tactics include m-44 sodium cyanide charges, steel-jaw traps, aerial shooting, neck snares, cage traps, burning and smoking out dens, spotlight shooting, shotgunning, leg and foot snares and a variety of poisons which frequently kill thousands of "non-target" species. All for the benefit of the livestock industry.

The ADC's chief eradication researcher on coyotes is Frederick Knowlton who heads the Millville Predator Research Facility and whose headquarters is an office at the University of Utah. The primary goal of Knowlton's research work is to develop techniques to totally control predator populations with poisons, traps and even tracking and eradication using radioactive isotopes. Knowlton has spent the last 30 years contributing directly to the killing of literally tens of thousands of coyotes. In a 1960's book on coyotes Knowlton is described on an aerial gunning campaign which downed two running coyotes. Upon landing and collecting the animals Knowlton comments with surprise at one of the coyotes which had only two legs, the other two having been ripped away in leghold traps. In the minds and hearts of the coyote nation there is a devil and his name is Fredrick Knowlton. Known to the environmental and animal movements for years the ADC has remained a bastillion of environmental and animal destruction in the US What manifest destiny has done to indigenous peoples in this country, ADC is doing to its indigenous wildlife.

As the fur farm wars raged with federal authorities and fur farmers on extreme red alert, an ALF council gathered in the Rocky Mountain wilderness to discuss the prospects of future guerilla campaigns. Warriors from three different bands expressed the need to escalate the defense of America's wildlife in the face of major repression and not to run and hide. Gathered around the council fire, federal documents detailing Knowlton's research were passed around in the firelight. With Federal police on all sides, any future attacks would have to be lightening fast, already our numbers were too reduced to risk the loss of even one warrior.

As a full moon rose over the encampment each warrior voiced his or her opinions on the path of war or retreat. When each had spoken, a final voice recounted the generations of death and destruction waged by ADC, and its impact on the nations of animals that had once roamed freely on these lands. In the distance a coyote's voice sang out, echoing in the warriors hearts sending shivers down their backs. It was decided the path would be war. As the old British ALF adage goes: "once it's decided, it's as good as done."

The next month, ALF moles were sent in the four directions recruiting warriors for this massive attack. While in Utah camouflage-clad "hikers" camped out above the Predator Research Facility spending long nights watching the movements of students and researchers on the compound. It was on one of these first nights that the raiders heard what would become a familiar sound. Each night wild coyotes from the nearby hills would sing their evening songs, in response most of the eighty captives would answer in unison in lonely heartfelt cries. The first time these songs penetrated the hearts of the hidden warriors, tears of sadness and rage would cloud their vision through binoculars as they pledged to avenge the dying coyotes in the pens below.

Back on the campus of the University of Utah at Logan (UofU), warriors dressed as college students were studying the courtyard office of Knowlton which stood just 50 yards from the University Police station in a dead end cul-de-sac. By October, the warriors were poised to strike. Gathered in a canyon far away from the Research Facility, ten warriors stood in a circle, each in their own uniforms for the night. For some university sweatshirts and daypacks and running shoes, while others wore thin ski-masks rolled above their eyes, camouflage shirts and pants and disposable hiking boots. Two others were dressed in nice dinner clothes. These were to be the drivers.

Topographical and highway street maps were given to the warriors in waterproof ziploc bags and enough unhandled cash in case of emergency, should separation be necessary for a fast escape. The drivers would be monitoring police scanners and each team would have radiocontact and hand relay signals between the warriors in each team should a call come in. In one warrior's pack was a suction glass remover and incendiary device for Knowlton's office. In another, boltcutters, wire cutters and thick gloves for the many holes that would need to cut in fences and coyote pens. One warrior, the lookout, held binoculars, spotting scope and an astronomy book; should this warrior be discovered, a stargazer was their alibi. The last warrior's pack was filled with another incendiary device, mini-mag flashlight with red lens and an assortment of tools that would be used to gain entry into the Predator Research Facility.

There was something very different about this raid. It was not seen as an offensive action, but a defensive one, not only on the coyotes behalf, but also for the warriors. Our movement was under attack, with human freedom as well as animal freedom at risk. Such an action was necessary to prove to our enemies that the ALF's back would not be broken.

Far away in downtown high-rises ATF and FBI agents worked feverishly around the clock attempting to eradicate the threat of an action like this one about to take place. Also, the long nights of recon had led the warriors to feel personally connected to the coyotes in the outdoor pens of the PRF. Many of these animals were born in the wild and knew the freedom others never had experienced. Each night the warriors would hear their cries and on some days would see coyotes in pens that had been intentionally starved for four days and then given poison-tainted feed knowing the coyote could not refuse food after this period of intentional starvation. Throughout the compound improvements could be seen being made as researchers attempted to expend their budgeted funding before their fiscal year was up. If a government agency did not spend its allotted funds, its budget might be reduced the next year rather then increased.

On one day Knowlton himself could be seen directing construction, while coyotes circled in pens surrounding him. Our attack would be focused on the Predator Research Facility building itself and the large outdoor enclosures that held over 40 coyotes. Another chain-link kennel building held at least 40 more coyotes but their location was too near the night watchman's house to risk liberation. Maybe if the facility was not on alert due to recent ALF raids the risk might be worth it, but to endanger the whole action most importantly the destruction of the Predator Research Facility for animals that sadly could be easily replaced, could not be justified. In most ALF actions the feelings of victory are often offset by the rage and frustration for having to leave animals behind. But if our action was successful, the destruction of the lab and Knowlton's research would mean the preservation of innumerable lives that would otherwise be extinguished by the benefits of ADC research.

Back on the UofU campus we would also attempt to strike Knowlton's office right beneath the University police's nose. On the evening of October 24th, two bicyclists pulled into a parking area on the u of u campus next to the Natural Resources Building, locked their bikes and walked arm in arm towards the police station near the courtyard that led to Knowlton's office. One of the cyclist's daypacks held a radio which was tuned to a channel monitored by a lookout with a police scanner. Establishing themselves with a clear view of the cop shop one warrior flashed the thumbs up while the other entered the dead end courtyard and approached the exterior window leading into Knowlton's office.

Pulling on a dark pair of coveralls, the warrior then removed the aluminum trim on the window holding the glass against its frame and used the suction cup device to remove the glass. On an earlier recon mission a "student" had banged on the glass hard enough to set off any alarm that might be connected to it, then withdrew to watch for any response. There wasn't one. The window was not alarmed. Setting the glass aside, the warrior rolled into the opening after lifting his daypack gingerly in. Emptying his pack of firestarting equipment and the incendiary device, he next filled the empty space with all of Knowlton's computer discs and other vital documents. Next he gathered books, desk drawers and other combustible materials and laid them around Knowlton's desk where the incendiary device was then placed setting the timer for shortly before dawn. The warrior then connected the 9-volt battery to the device thereby engaging it and gazing around him, took one last look at the office of a man whose career was based on the annihilation of a species.

No radio transmissions had been made which indicated the all-clear. Just 35 minutes after having entered the office, the warrior fled gathering the computer discs and other bounty. Stripping off his coveralls, the warrior then walked past the lookout's location just 100 feet from the police station. The two then walked back to their locked mountain bikes and rode away into the night. At about the same time as Knowlton's office was being visited, a single file line of six warriors jogged along a path in the forest lands that led to the boundary fence of the Predator Research Facility and outlying coyote pens. The sky was magnificently filled with stars, and as the warriors approached the furthest fence, the lookout broke off to climb a rise where contact would be established with another lookout in the drop-off and pick-up vehicle. Climbing the ridge the lookout could see all roads entering into the ADC compound as well as the watchman's house and coyote pens.

At the fence the remaining five warriors followed the lead warrior who began to cut a hole in the boundary fence in which to enter through. Once inside the fenceline, the warriors broke into two groups, one which would free the coyotes while the others would raid the lab. Crawling on their bellies, two warriors approached the Predator Research Facility. Climbing one last chain-link fence the warriors were now deep within the ADC compound and only a stone's throw from the sleeping watchman's window. An alarm test had been made on a small bathroom window with success and now the warriors approached the window and began to remove the screen and frame. At this point too much noise was being made to continue, so the warriors contemplated other points of entry that would create less noise as precious minutes ticked by. Finally as if on cue, the coyotes in the nearby kennel building began to howl and cry offering enough noise cover to rip the window from its frame.

Entering the PRF, the warriors were immediately faced with dozens of coyote skulls, leghold traps and "do not feed" signs outside the laboratory bathroom. Crawling on hands and knees, one warrior went straight for the structural center of the laboratory while the other gathered more computer discs and photo slides. The two warriors could have spent hours leafing through the files of predator research, but time was not something they had a lot of. After the stolen records in Michigan were recovered and their shipment used as a lead to a safe house, the decision was made to destroy the research at the PRF, not just seize it.

Setting the incendiary device amidst a pile of traps and desk drawers and other wooden materials the warriors activated the device and quickly exited the building. The incendiary device in the prf was scheduled to go off at the exact time as the device in Knowlton's office. Retreating quietly back to the outlying coyote pens the two warriors regrouped with the three warriors cutting gaping holes in coyote pens. The warriors were each carrying a pair of boltcutters and excitedly described how coyotes were approaching the fence and digging opposite the warriors as they cut through the fence only inches away from the coyotes in an obvious attempt to speed their release. Stepping back, the coyotes were quick to follow each other out the pens and toward the mountains where wild coyotes could be heard calling to them.

As the five warriors cut fence after fence, coyotes in groups of twos and threes could be seen escaping the pens and racing to freedom. When the last pen was emptied the warriors retreated single file back towards the hills themselves. By the time they regrouped with the lookout on the ridge the warriors had already called for the rendezvous pick-up driver to come, so the six warriors quietly padded down the same path they had entered as the star-filled sky was filled with the songs of coyotes disappearing into the mountain wilderness.

As the first signs of dawn shone grey in the night sky, the incendiary devices triggered in both the UofU office of Fred Knowlton and at the Predator Research Facility. On the campus, it wasn't long before the police noticed smoke billowing from the Natural Resources Building and quickly extinguished the fire but not before years of research went up in smoke. The firefighters own water had caused much of the damage. As the firefighters on campus doused the flames of Knowlton's office the call came in from the watchman that the PRF was ablaze. By the time firefighters reached the facility over half of the laboratory had been completely destroyed. A week later, the whole structure would be determined unsafe and the entire lab was demolished. In January of 1993 Fred Knowlton was still pleading with county planning commissioners to grant him a temporary building permit to construct a new lab. All research at the USd.a.'s Predator Research Facility had ground to a halt.

To add further insult to injury, the ALF accused Knowlton of illegally dumping tons of radioactive contaminated coyote carcasses from field experiments in New Mexico and when he denied the allegation the ALF provided an investigative reporter with his own memo to another researcher admitting his knowledge of not having obtained the necessary permits before burying his dead research subjects. Thirtythree coyotes meanwhile were never recovered and the researchers were quick to express their concerns that the animals could not survive in the wild, but we know better don't we? Running from the torture chambers of Knowlton's lab that night the escaping coyotes saw not six human figures trotting down a mountain path, but six wild coyote warriors who had not forgotten their four-legged brothers and sisters.

Days later at a remote hideout victory campfires blazed as Knowlton's computer discs were fed to the flames by the ALF warriors who had confiscated them from his office. Once more the ALF had proven that what could not be accomplished with years of protest, could be achieved with a handful of brave-hearted warriors. Now it was time to wait for others to follow our lead.

CHAPTER FOURTEEN
The Story of Coyote Nations (just one chapter...)

Hey is that you? Sitting there on the hill? Watching us tonight?
Have you come to let us out of here? We've been waiting for you.
Crying every night.
Trying to tell you hoping you would come.
Have you heard... what they are doing to us in here? Listen, 140 coyote people crying in
distress. Each with their own story of separation, pain, torture and death.
Listen, they are trying to tell you, enough to break your heart. All true.

Brother. You got to let us out of here.
Warrior, listen in case you're questioning your next move.
They starve us in here, then tempt us with sheep, radioactive poison sheep.
And they watch us die. Feeding our pain into a computer to study.
Sister-warrior listen, in case you are unsure.
They mate us to have pups, then steal them, maim them, poison them, we never see them
again. Only sometimes we hear them, only children.
They cut us open, take our wombs, poison us, watch us die, see if we can still have pups.
And when they are done with us, they dump our bodies by the ton, in mass toxic grave.

Lightning-womyn sister of mine, let us out.
Thunder-man brother, pay them back.
We are Coyote, and our medicine is strong, even now.
You and I, we are the same. You Coyote Warrior, we Coyote. Spirit healers.
It is our way, always wild, never die.
Morning has come and you are leaving, our hearts are sad, and we cry to you.
But we listen to your promise to return.

Hey its you again! You are back!
This time you stand tall, proud, brave hearts forward as you walk the road.
Not come to watch. To act!
We see you there, cutting fence with their tools.
Coming closer, we sing, coyotes in distress, coyotes excited.
We are sick, and our tribes broken, but tonight some will go free.
We howl. One heart together with you, to give strength to our weak, love to the ones left
behind, hearts break, crying in sorrow.

Run Coyote. Head to the hills. Run and be free. Be Coyote again.
Do not look back.
We hear your warrior cries, you are strong, and use our medicine well.
You take heart from us, and we from you.
Still there are some that are our sisters, brothers, all star soldiers.

Maybe we will make it… at least some.
Coyote Warriors where are you tonight?

Today we watched the laboratory burn. The one where our torturers hide.
We watched the flames as the sun came up, danced and sang like Coyote again.
Now we must run, and so must you. But forever, our hearts shall be as one.

Hey Coyote Warriors! Where are you? We've been looking for you.
We need you. We wait for you in the deserts, mountains, plains, our home.
You Coyote Warriors belong here too.
Born to the humans, still living among them in their crazy cities.
The time for you to leave is now. Come home. There is much to be done.
Many of our wild ones still imprisoned, remember?
Being tortured, killed, destroyed. We never forget.
Yours is to fight, this fight dog soldier. Keep our wild spirits alive!
Sacred hoop strong, it was never broken.

And your home is here, among us your wild sisters and brothers.
We have much to teach you, remind you of our power. Come home Coyote Warriors. It is
time to reweave the web, the tribe to each other, all to the Earth Mother.
Build your fires, and there we will sing to you. Tell you of the days long ago, when we
were all one. Coyote medicine is your strength.
The earth spirits are strong, and are poised to help you… if you listen.

Warrior societies, your time is now. Find each other. Come back home.
You should only be among the enemy to raid.
All you warriors, keepers of the dream, do not let them have you.
Do not go down.
What makes you think you do not have to hide? We must.
We have coyote medicine to help you stay free.
Remember what it is like to live.
Wild. Proud. Together. Free.
Prepare earth warriors.
Trickster is coming.

CHAPTER FIFTEEN
Epilogue for Operation Bite Back

*O*ut of the ashes of the Predator Research Facility came retaliation from the FBI, as animal researchers and fur farmers organized lobbying efforts, screaming for an end to the ALF attacks on their legitimate businesses. Within two weeks of the Utah raid Jonathan Paul was jailed on contempt of court charges for not providing information to the ongoing Federal Grand Juries which were now convened in Oregon, Washington, Michigan, Louisiana and Utah, all hunting for ALF warriors. No sooner had Paul been released from jail, then Rik Scarce took his place. When Scarce was released still tight-lipped, he was followed by Deb Stout and then Kim Trimiew as Federal investigators used the Grand Jury process to intimidate activists into giving information about the ALF as too little physical evidence existed to indict anyone other than Coronado.

It could be argued that the grand jury was being used to harass a political movement, but with ALF attacks such as Operation Bite Back the Federal government could legitimize its witch hunts as investigations of "serious criminal activity". US authorities began to cooperate with Canadian authorities who were conducting their own investigations of the ALF after 29 cats had been rescued from a University in Alberta. One of the supporting activists from that raid had testified against the ALF and a warrant was soon issued for David Barbarash a known ALF supporter and former member, and Darren Thurston another ALF supporter. In early 1994, David Barbarash was captured in Scotts Valley, California leaving Jonathan Paul's home. Paul, a known associate of Coronado's had been under federal surveillance since his release from jail. Barbarash was soon extradited to Canada to face ALF charges in Alberta. He would spend over 20 months in prison for his "crimes" of rescuing cats destined to be killed by vivisectors, as would Darren Thurston.

It would be nice to believe that in 1993 and '94 ALF warriors were sheltered by the animal rights and radical environmental movements as the Federal Government hunted for them, but such was not the case. By harassing, subpoenaing and jailing innocent activists the FBI successfully drove a wedge between the ALF and its previous supporters. Many activists were witnessing the repercussions of supporting the ALF and one by one were made uneasy and afraid to offer assistance to ALF activists on the run. In classic divide and conquer tactics, the US Government punished the legitimate animal rights and liberation movement as well as many Earth First! activists knowing by doing so they would turn many of these people against the ALF. It was a tactic that had been successfully used against every resistance movement opposed to US policy. It would only be a matter of time before the pressure exerted on ALF supporters, activists and their families and friends would bring to the surface information that would lead to the arrest of an ALF warrior.

CHAPTER SIXTEEN
The Capture of Rod Coronado

*O*n September 28, 1994 Martin Rubio was feeding his animals on the Pascua Yaqui Indian Reservation outside of Tucson, Arizona when a tribal police car pulled up to his house. A Caucasian officer approached Rubio requesting his aid in helping a wounded redtail hawk that had been brought into the tribal fire department. The request was not unusual as, since his arrival on the reservation two years before, Rubio had been active in many community projects and his fondness of animals was known to many. Entering the tribal fire department Rubio was immediately jumped by over 12 agents from the FBI, ATF and US Marshals.

Rod Coronado had been captured. Labeled as "armed and dangerous" despite an ATF background check that revealed the ownership of no firearms. Coronado had been living peaceably with the tribe of his origins organizing activities for the youth in his community and doing grassroots organizing with the Student Environmental Action Coalition and local human rights groups as well as cultural preservation work for the Pascua Yaqui Tribe.

An anonymous tip to Crimestoppers led to Coronado's capture and a $22,000 reward was paid out to the informant by fur farmers, taxidermists, big game hunters and vivisectors. Bail was denied and in the first week of November, Coronado was extradited to Michigan to be arraigned on a two-count indictment relating to the ALF raid on MSU. The evidence used to indict Coronado was his own writings and news interviews voicing support of Operation Bite Back as well as phone records and a Federal Express billing slip found in the box of stolen research materials from MSU vivisector Aulerich's office that placed him in Michigan during the raid. Handwriting analysis also had matched the writing on the label to Coronado's.

In early December, Coronado was granted bail after a lengthy court battle with US Attorneys, FBI and ATF agents in which prosecutors argued for his continued detention based on the fact that he was a flight risk and still a fugitive from justice for illegal direct actions in three other countries, Canada, Iceland, and Denmark. His bond was set at an incredible $650,000.00. Just before his release from federal custody, Coronado was offered a plea agreement in which he was offered the lesser charge of a felony with a maximum of an 18-month sentence, if he agreed to testify as to who sent him to Michigan to act as an ALF conduit for stolen materials. Coronado flatly refused and was later released on bond. Within a month, a superseding seven count indictment was issued accusing Coronado of organizing the complete Operation Bite Back campaign, this despite the ATF and FBI knowing many others were involved. Federal prosecutors strategized that if all the weight of prosecution was laid on Coronado, he could possibly be coerced to testify rather than face 10 to 12 years in prison alone if found guilty. Other evidence, a reconstructed typewriter ribbon found in Coronado's storage locker in Oregon requesting funding for ALF attacks being the most incriminating, and phone records that placed Coronado near ALF targets close to the time raids took place, was leveled against him. In addition federal investigators had matched Coronado's finger prints to an empty museum case from which a Seventh Cavalryman's Journal from the Little Bighorn Battlefield was stolen. A press release followed the theft demanding the return of sacred objects on display and an equal amount of space in the museum to communicate the indigenous perspective of "Custer's Last Stand". Prosecutors threatened to indict Coronado in Montana on separate charges. Prosecutors were also hoping to use DNA tests to match Coronado's saliva to that found on a cigarette butt that was used as a delay timer on an incendiary device that malfunctioned at the Fur Breeders Co-op in Sandy, Utah in September of 1991.

The court case would be heard in the Western District of Michigan which meant that the jury pool would be the predominantly white suburbs and agricultural area of Western Michigan. Federal prosecutors had decided to prosecute Coronado in Michigan, far away from the west which in their eyes meant a liberal jury and also away from Washington where the FBI and ATF were being criticized severely due to their murder of Vicki Weaver and her son in Ruby Ridge, Washington, in a botched FBI/ATF, US Marshals raid. Coronado's dilemma was that if he went to trial he would have to convince the jury why he wrote a letter asking for funding to attack fur farms and why he was always nearby ALF targets just before raids as well as blatantly lie and testify that he was not a member of the ALF. He would also be put on the stand and undoubtedly be questioned by the prosecution about his connections with other activists. Any denial of facts known already to the FBI could cost further charges of perjury as well as providing the Government with information that could lead to the indictment of others. Coronado always felt an obligation to accept responsibility for his own actions. The history of indigenous resistance and environmental protection in the US had taught Coronado to never expect justice from a judicial system that favored big business and private property over the environment, animals and indigenous peoples. A Native American tried by an all white jury for crimes he refused to condemn was almost certainly destined for conviction. Not to mention the risk of other activists being called to testify which would be the bait for information that might lead to further indictments of suspected ALF warriors. Meanwhile the biomedical and animal agriculture industries were demanding Coronado's head on a plate as a symbol of deterrence to other remaining ALF warriors. The US Attorney prosecuting the case had made Coronado's conviction his priority, setting aside all other cases of his until he had it. It was at this time prosecutors once more told Coronado he could testify against other ALF members, receive a maximum of an 18 month sentence of which he would only serve eight months and be done with it all. Coronado still refused. Instead he began plea negotiations to avoid going to trial. Coronado was willing to testify as to his own role in the ALF, but refused to incriminate others.

In March of 1995 Coronado entered a guilty plea to two counts, aiding and abetting the arson at MSU. For receiving stolen materials from the raid and a charge of destruction of US Government property for his theft of the Cavalryman's Journal. In return he was absolved of all federal prosecution in the US districts investigating the ALF and promised never to be subpoenaed, questioned or indicted on charges relating to Operation Bite Back. A specific component of his plea bargain was that he would not be required to testify against other activists.

Some activists in the animal rights movement were quick to criticize Coronado for his unwillingness to go to trial and use the courts as a platform for the ALF. Others including many ALF supporters in England felt that Coronado should do whatever was necessary short of testifying, to obtain a short prison sentence. For many it was easy to say what they felt Coronado should do, yet few of us can say what we would do when faced with as much as 12 years in prison. Without a doubt Coronado has proven that he is worth more to the earth and animals out of prison than in it. Any people willing to criticize Coronado should first ask themselves why they didn't support the ALF during Operation Bite Back, let alone participate then or now in ALF actions. Many of us in the ALF knew that the only thing that stood between the FBI and the ALF was Coronado's unwillingness to testify about his role with other ALF members. The reason the US Attorneys had first focused their case on Coronado was not because they believed he was criminally responsible for all of Operation Bite Back, though physical evidence was convincing that he was integral, but mainly because he was willing to give voice to a movement that was currently threatening the multi-billion dollar industries of animal abuse and environmental destruction through means that the US Government had no control over.

On August 11, 1995 Coronado was sentenced to 57 months in Federal Prison before a courtroom full of vivisectors and FBI and ATF agents after the judge heard testimony as to the devastating impact the ALF had had on the animal research community. The judge compared Coronado to the Oklahoma City Bombers and despite his acknowledgement of Coronado's "proven rehabilitation" as seen in his two years of community service on the Pascua Yaqui Reservation, he stated that a detrimental sentence was needed to serve as a deterrent to other people willing to break the law for what they believed in. The judge refused to award Coronado a reduced sentence based on his own acceptance of responsibility stating that his refusal to cooperate with law enforcement prevented it, this action alone cost Coronado an additional 18 months. In addition to the 4-½ years in prison the judge also ordered that Coronado pay $2.5 million in restitution to the victims of Operation Bite Back, to be paid in full immediately. To add insult to injury, US Attorneys wrote a letter to Coronado two days after his sentencing asking him why he was willing to protect members of the animal rights community who wouldn't even show their support by attending his sentencing. The only people present in the courtroom in Coronado's defense were his parents, members of the Pascua Yaqui Tribe, and members of the People of Color Caucus of the Student Environmental Action Coalition. Still Coronado refused the latest offer and until 1999 will be a prisoner of war from the US Governments continued war against nature and animals. On September 11, 1995 Coronado surrendered at the Federal Prison in Safford, Arizona and became the first ALF warrior in US history to be sent to Federal Prison for actions on behalf of earth and animals.

CHAPTER SEVENTEEN
Brave Hearts Forward!

*N*ineteen ninety-seven; it is a felony to free animals from laboratories, fur farms, factory farms, zoos and rodeos. Punishment up to ten years in prison, fines up to $100,000. Release one mink back into its native habitat from a fur farm and you are a terrorist with a $100,000 price on your head. Welcome to a country where politicians are bought and paid for, where the agenda of the Justice Department is decided by big business and corporate dollars, the largest US industries being the food, medical, military and construction trades whose very existence is based on earth destruction and animal exploitation. Billions of dollars of profits from misery, death and destruction. Earth, animal and human life – all just another commodity in the "Free" world.

Warriors! it is time to step forward, be brave, act from our hearts and not let the fear of our enemies or what they can do to our physical bodies stop us from doing what we know is right. It is time for you to stop pointing fingers at others, quick to reveal what is wrong with their path of struggle. Make change with your own lives, not by trying to change that of others. Real change comes from within, it is not something you can achieve by buying t-shirts or putting a bumpersticker on your ozone destroying, animal tested-gasoline-powered car.

Spreading an idea is good, but it takes warriors to lead this battle to defend what remains of earth and animals. The fact that there is little or no justice for the earth and animals should come as no surprise to anyone who knows US history. Yet still we plod on, hoping that we can scrape a few meager crumbs together through legislative reform or corporate compassion. History tells us that all this has ever done is allowed the spirit of resistance to become harnessed, tuned into "politically correct" consumption of products that still make our enemies richer and stronger. Turning our power over to others who delegate themselves as the leaders of our movements, ranking in five-figure salaries while they compromise the earth and animals they claim to represent.

When we as warriors appoint ourselves as guardians of all that is natural and free, we accept the responsibility to act on the earth's and our nonhuman relations behalf as if it was our own flesh and blood. We do not replace the vivisector with the friendly needle of a "compassionate killer". We do not measure our victories by column length coverage or length of broadcast on the corporate controlled media machine, but by our commitment to ensure that those that we rescue and that which we defend is protected from our enemies with our own bodies and freedom as shields if necessary. We do not slander those who have sacrificed their freedom and risked their lives because their beliefs do not reflect our own. We show great respect, not only to our Earth Mother and her Animal Children but also to each other. We are warriors. The rear guard who must defend the weak, sick and voiceless who cannot defend themselves against the evil that many humans have become. There are too few of us, and we must not let ourselves be divided by idealistic virtues when we are all willing to risk our lives and freedom for earth and animals. Like the indigenous nations of this land who often warred with each other, yet came together when the threat against the earth was upon us, we must also put aside our differences and concentrate on the common enemies we all share. Like the many tribes who differed from one another yet all shared great reverence and respect for mother earth, we must also recognize our differences and choose carefully who we want to live and fight with, but come together as one solid strong ungovernable force when the enemy is upon us and as we witness the sin of animal abuse and earth destruction. Our orders are from our Creator and we need to find solutions to the problems that keep us apart and join together to achieve the victories we all believe in.

We also must recognize that we are living in a state of martial law where information is controlled to the extent that we may never receive the support we would like in protecting the environment and animals which ultimately benefit all life. For these reasons we must not be discouraged when simply fighting to ensure a healthy planet earth that can sustain life is seen by the governing powers as acts of terrorism. But remember, the one greatest thing that separates us from our enemies is our reverence for life. All Life. Even the lives of our enemies. Destroying the machines of destruction rather than those who operate them must always remain our prime objective. That and rescuing the victims of that destruction with guarantees of their safety and sanctuary. If we do this, our earth powers will never leave us and the spirit of love and compassion will return to the face of the earth.

We have to remember that the battle on behalf of mother earth and her animals is about love. There's enough hate in the world generated by our opposition. To perpetuate more violence on behalf of our cause only reduces us to the enemy's evil depths. I know its hard, when the things we see can be so cruel and callous, but when we become motivated out of the dark force of hate we step closer to becoming just another political faction justifying violence to achieve its means. As the revolutionary Che' Guevera once said, "Let me say at the risk of sounding ridiculous, that the true revolutionary is motivated by immense feelings of love."

Some people within the animal rights and environmental movements believe that to achieve our goals we must present our ideas in such a way as to appeal to mainstream society, that with public support we can legislate change and influence our political representatives to see us not as a threat, but as harbingers of a new age. These people will say it is counterproductive to their agenda to burn laboratories down, and destroy animal research records, and that the ALF and other direct action groups are extreme and are jeopardizing everything that has been accomplished for the environment and animals through legitimate means. We say absolutely. Why accept larger and cleaner cages for lab animals and the preservation of the Wolf, Grizzly and Condor with "experimental nonessential populations"? We demand nothing short of the total abolition of vivisection and the complete protection of the last remaining native wildlife and their habitat. Yes it is extreme to burn labs, but the ALF is answering to an extreme situation. We didn't escalate the war against nature, the enemy has and we are only here to fight it. What is extreme is what the governing forces of this continent have done to those peaceful nations of others called animals that humanity lived in harmony with for thousands of years before European Conquest. The crumbs from the political tables of compromise will not achieve liberation of our mother earth and her animals, they will only result in false faith in a political and corporate structure that cannot survive without animal and earth abuse. So to the apologist of the animal rights and environmental organizations who are quick to denounce the defense of earth and animals to preserve their position and favor by our enemies we say, we are warriors, nothing more, nothing less. The ALF leaves the path of moderation to those who sincerely believe that that is the road to victory.

But we also ask that those who approach the legal means of reform with the same conviction in which the ALF approaches its own, not be so quick to condemn the avenues of illegal direct action. Without illegal action on the path in pursuit of liberty and justice, many of this century's greatest social changes never would have been achieved. As with any struggle for social and especially ecological change, all avenues of action must be utilized and recognized because without them our battle appears to be that of a splintered faction unable to share basic common goals. The animal rights and liberation movements must readily accept ALF cells as its belligerent force, in the same way as many other revolutionary bodies across the world who reflect the objectives of a larger, yet more moderate movement that share the same goals.

Not only do we rescue individuals and utilize guerilla warfare to sabotage industries destroying earth and animals, but whether others recognize it or not, the ALF also brings issues to light and creates the catalyst for others in the movement to continue pressuring for change. Actions speak louder than words, and those actions lead to more talk which breeds more action.

Ultimately, direct action is only temporary liberation. It is the immediate liberation of a few and the unleashing of a vision that requires lifelong commitment to achieve lasting change. A commitment that will undoubtedly lead to great personal sacrifice, knowing true peace and justice may be years in coming. We must always be searching for solutions to the problems we see in today's society and live our ideals not only towards the earth mother and animals, but also towards other humans whether we wear the mask of the ALF or not. Its not as simple as a choice in diet, though that's a start, but involves the willingness to listen and understand others whose views we might at first be unwilling to accept. Only through that process will our direct action movement diversify and grow while never losing its integrity.

These thoughts and views have grown within us as one ALF cell which has survived police repression, underground resistance and in-fighting amongst above-ground movement supporters. What we have realized is the path of animal liberation invariably leads to the wider road of human and earth liberation. A road that is filled with brave-hearted warriors of all sexual persuasions, races, religions and beliefs, yet all traveling forward towards the same light which is true victory. So here we are survivors ourselves, carrying the scars not only of barbed wire and broken glass but scars from the heartless actions of men who know not what they do. Still, we will never give up. We do not have that choice, we must constantly think of the future generations and the earth they will inherit. And on this day we are inspired. In our darkest moments we have seen others take on the warrior path and the light at the end of the tunnel is growing into a brilliant blaze fed by the spirits of young warriors who are the hope of millions of oppressed animals and our wounded mother earth. One day we will be able to gather around the council fire and remove our masks to reveal the faces of the human spirit that in the past lived in harmony with all life. Until that day may the long cold nights of ALF warriors the world over be filled with the light of protection, the strength of all past earth warriors and the powers of nature which we fight for. Our enemies strength lies in the force of fear which shall be overcome with the power of love. Love for our Mother Earth, love for her Animal Children, love for each other and love for the spirit of resistance. We know in our hearts what is right we must have the courage to follow it. Now, Brave Hearts Forward!, Coward Hearts To The Rear!

ANIMAL LIBERATION FRONT OF NORTH AMERICA WESTERN WILDLIFE UNIT